Fair Trade Without the Froth

WITHDRAWN

Fair Trade Without the Froth

A Dispassionate Economic Analysis of
'Fair Trade'

SUSHIL MOHAN

The Institute of Economic Affairs

First published in Great Britain in 2010 by
The Institute of Economic Affairs
2 Lord North Street
Westminster
London sw1p 3lb
in association with Profile Books Ltd

The mission of the Institute of Economic Affairs is to improve public
understanding of the fundamental institutions of a free society, by analysing
and expounding the role of markets in solving economic and social problems.

A CIP catalogue record for this book is available from the British Library.

ISBN 978 0 255 36645 8

Many IEA publications are translated into languages other than English or
are reprinted. Permission to translate or to reprint should be sought from the
Director General at the address above.

Typeset in Stone by MacGuru Ltd
info@macguru.org.uk

Printed and bound in Great Britain by Hobbs the Printers

CONTENTS

THE AUTHOR

Dr Sushil Mohan is an applied economist with research interests in issues relating to the interaction between agricultural commodity trade and economic development. He has published several papers on the problem of price risk faced by coffee producers in developing countries and how they can manage this risk. He has also published on the benefits for developing countries from reforming their agricultural trade. Sushil worked for over ten years at key levels in trade promotion agencies in London and India. He served as Consultant for the Commonwealth Secretariat for developing the coffee industry in the Republic of Vanuatu; as Board Member (1993–7) of the UK Tea Council, International Tea Committee and International Coffee Organisation; and in the Commerce Ministry of India dealing with trade policy and development.

FOREWORD

The success of the Fair Trade movement has created an intense debate in recent years. It has come under attack – especially from believers in free markets – for deviating from the practice of free trade that has led so many people to emerge from poverty in recent years. In turn, many of the proponents of Fair Trade passionately denounce free trade and big business, despite their obvious contribution to reductions in poverty. This monograph is to be commended for taking a dispassionate look at the subject. Indeed, it finds that this particular line of argument is a dead end. Fair Trade arises from the free choices of producers and consumers: it is therefore very much a niche part of the system of free trade. The basic principle of Fair Trade is that the organisations involved label products (such as coffee, bananas and so on) for which the producers fulfil certain conditions in the production process. These conditions generally include, for example, not employing child labour. The producers also receive a premium above the market price for the product, as well as some form of price guarantee should the market price fall below a particular level. Consumers buy the products freely knowing that producers are being treated 'fairly'. None of this deviates from the principles of free trade – even if it were the case that the choices that consumers make to buy Fair Trade products are misguided.

Having established that Fair Trade products do not

intrinsically deviate from the principles of free trade, the author then moves on to examine the claims of Fair Trade's proponents. This examination is justified – indeed overdue. The claims that Fair Trade activists make are strong; the public esteem for the movement is very high; yet there is hardly any serious empirical analysis of the movement's claims. Indeed, even this study stops short of a detailed, comprehensive and conclusive analysis because the data simply do not exist to test the arguments of Fair Trade advocates.

The evidence that is gathered in this monograph, however, does show that the claims of proponents of the Fair Trade movement are probably exaggerated. There are many other ways in which the benefits that Fair Trade brings to producers can be obtained – some of those ways have long been embedded in conventional trade. Furthermore, it is not clear that Fair Trade benefits the poorest producers, and the administration and fees involved in becoming a certified producer are not trivial. The main claims that the Fair Trade organisations make relating to their ability to protect producers from price instability are exaggerated: few consumers will realise that, although there is a price guarantee through Fair Trade, there is no guarantee of the quantity that can be sold at that price.

At the same time, the author finds that the claims of Fair Trade's detractors are also exaggerated. Theoretical problems with the model (for example, that it encourages overproduction) that are not serious problems in practice will often be brought up.

Those who read this monograph hoping for a wholesale denunciation of the Fair Trade movement will be disappointed. Rightly, the author concludes on the basis of the limited evidence. Nevertheless, the author's nuanced position should itself be a huge challenge to Fair Trade's supporters. Fair Trade is not, the author finds, a long-term strategy for development; the objectives of Fair Trade are often fulfilled in conventional markets; the Fair Trade rhetoric is not generally justified; the costs for producers of being involved in labelling initiatives are not inconsiderable; and there are many other labelling initiatives with overt social objectives (such as the protection of rainforest). These other initiatives may suffer as a result of attempts by the Fair Trade movement to ensure that Fair Trade schools, parishes and so on use products with the particular Fairtrade label as opposed to other labels.

Overall, this monograph is an important contribution to a debate that tends to generate more heat than light. It is a long-overdue, dispassionate analysis of the Fair Trade movement.

PHILIP BOOTH

Editorial and Programme Director, Institute of Economic Affairs

Professor of Insurance and Risk Management, Cass Business School,

City University

September 2010

SUMMARY

- Fair Trade is part of the market economy and is not, in any way, in opposition to free trade. Fair Trade sales have grown enormously in the last few years.
- Fair Trade brings certain benefits to producers, such as guaranteed prices, a social premium and the enforcement of particular labour conditions.
- These benefits may not be as great as many of Fair Trade's proponents imply. For example, if the market price falls below the guaranteed price level, though the guaranteed price will be paid for any Fair Trade purchases, the quantity of produce that will be bought from the producer is not guaranteed.
- The benefits of Fair Trade also come at a cost. There is a levy on the wholesaler as well as a certification charge for producers. The certification charge starts at £1,570 in the first year – a huge sum of money for producers in the poorest countries.
- Fair Trade does not focus on the poorest countries. Fair Trade penetration is greater in middle-income than in poor countries.
- Criticisms of Fair Trade are also exaggerated. At its current level of penetration it is likely to do little harm in terms of distorting markets.

- The benefits claimed by Fair Trade can also be obtained from the normal business relationships that exist between primary product producers and buyers. Attempts by proponents of Fair Trade to denigrate free trade and normal market practices are not helpful and distort realities.
- Primary product producers will often gain much more by selling speciality brands of their product than they will from adopting the Fair Trade label.
- Many other social labelling initiatives exist with objectives that are different from and often more transparent than those of Fair Trade. Attempts by Fair Trade to require schools, parishes and so on to stock Fair Trade goods can damage other social labelling initiatives or require very poor producers to suffer the bureaucracy and costs of obtaining multiple labels.
- Fair Trade is not a long-term development strategy, and the model is not appropriate for all producers. It is also unable to address structural problems within trading systems. Fair Trade's proponents need to show some humility and accept that it is a niche market designed to benefit some producers; nevertheless, it does achieve that limited objective.

TABLE

Fair Trade Without the Froth

1 THE THEORY OF FAIR TRADE

Introduction

The growth of the Fair Trade[1] market is both unique and controversial. Fair Trade products sell for a higher price than comparable conventional products without delivering any extra physical quality. The Fair Trade movement campaigns to grow its market – sometimes in an aggressive way using the vehicle of its staunch supporters. Fair Trade claims to address social and environmental problems and injustices exacerbated by conventional trading in global markets, and it tends to blame 'unjust' market relationships for low commodity prices and the hardships endured by subsistence producers and workers in the developing world. Fair Trade campaigning tends to convey the impression that its success is contingent upon increasing consumer awareness of what it would describe as the exploitative nature of conventional global trade and multinational corporations. Fair Trade enthusiasts participate in protests highlighting these issues, though lately such protests have been diluted because

---

[1] There is some difficulty in determining exactly how to use the term 'Fair Trade'. In general, as this monograph will have an international audience, I will use the term 'Fair Trade' to refer to a product certified by some kind of body which demands certain conditions of and/or makes particular guarantees to the producers of the relevant products. 'Fairtrade' will be used to refer to products certified by the Fairtrade Foundation in the UK.

of the increasing participation of large corporations in the Fair Trade movement.

The Fair Trade claims and protestations draw reactions from commentators who believe in the many virtues of international trade and free market mechanisms, including the critical role they can play in improving the conditions of poor producers and workers in underdeveloped countries. In addition, a number of commentators have misgivings about the vision and practices of Fair Trade. Consequently, as the visibility of Fair Trade has grown over the years, so have the debates between its advocates and critics about its benefits and detriments. These debates raise certain important questions. Can Fair Trade lead to significant benefits for producers and workers in developing countries? Are these benefits worth the costs imposed by Fair Trade certification? Are these benefits available in other, perhaps more efficient, ways? Are Fair Trade's claims that conventional international trade is unjust for producers and workers in developing countries overblown? Is Fair Trade an 'enterprise' solution to global poverty or an attempt to undermine a system of free trade?

The objective of this monograph is to analyse the theory and practice of Fair Trade in order to provide insights into these questions. It emerges that Fair Trade is a niche speciality marketing device within the free market system for increasing the welfare of a target group. It is wrong for proponents of Fair Trade to campaign to correct the so-called injustices of global trade or to suggest that Fair Trade can correct apparent injustices. Such campaigning undermines the role of conventional international trade and other market-based mechanisms that offer immense possibilities for the world's poorest people.

The monograph is organised as follows. This chapter outlines the main features, history, institutions and sales profile of Fair Trade. Chapter 2 examines the extent to which Fair Trade is different from or similar to free trade. Chapter 3 evaluates the benefits and detriments of Fair Trade. Chapter 4 explores alternative mechanisms that also claim to promote fair business practices and sustainable production. Chapter 5 discusses, based on the evidence examined in the previous chapters, whether Fair Trade is a sustainable long-run strategy for development and for assisting marginalised producers and workers in developing countries.

What is Fair Trade?

Fair Trade is an organised social movement which promotes environmental and labour standards and social policy objectives in areas related to the production and trading of Fair Trade labelled and unlabelled goods. Its strategic intent is to use market-based strategies to mobilise consumer awareness to help marginalised producers and workers move from a position of vulnerability to greater economic security. It does so without being involved directly in commodity production or trade but by offering producers and workers particular forms of market structure and contractual terms that bring particular benefits to them. It focuses in particular on exports from developing countries to developed countries. The most widely recognised definition of Fair Trade was crafted in 2001 by the FINE, an umbrella organisation of Fair Trade networks:

> Fair Trade is a trading partnership, based on dialogue,
> transparency and respect, which seeks greater equity
> in international trade. It contributes to sustainable
> development by offering better trading conditions to,

and securing the rights of, marginalized producers and workers – especially in the South. Fair Trade organizations (backed by consumers) are engaged actively in supporting producers, awareness raising and in campaigning for changes in the rules and practice of conventional international trade.

It should be noted that this definition explicitly mentions political goals: Fair Trade is not simply a product-certification movement.

While this definition states the general principles of Fair Trade, there are a number of more precise characteristics of Fair Trade certified products:

- Traders pay producers an agreed minimum price that covers the costs of sustainable production and living; this gives way to the market price whenever the latter is above this minimum.
- Traders should, in addition to the minimum price, also provide a social premium, of around 5 to 10 per cent, for development and technical assistance.
- Fair Trade products must respect a series of social and environmental criteria.[2]
- Traders, as far as possible, must purchase directly from producers or producer organisations using long-term contracts to lessen the number of intermediaries and to promote long-term planning and stability.

---

2   Fair Trade producers and those involved in the Fair Trade products supply chain must follow standards regarding working conditions, wages, child labour and the environment. These include adherence to the International Labour Organisation (ILO) agreements, such as those banning child and slave labour, guaranteeing a safe workplace and the right to unionise, adherence to the United Nations charter of human rights, and protection and conservation of the environment.

- Traders should help provide producers with credit of up to 60 per cent of the value purchased when requested.

To ensure that Fair Trade labelled products comply with these prescriptions, they must come from Fair Trade inspected and certified producers or producer organisations and the supply chain must also have been monitored by Fair Trade organisations. The Fairtrade Labelling Organizations International (FLO), which is responsible for regulating Fair Trade certification standards and labelling for individual products, stipulates the minimum criteria such as price and premium calculations as well as contract and payment conditions that the trading process must fulfil in order for each product to be labelled and sold as Fair Trade. There may be some variations in Fair Trade certification procedures between products and organisations (large farm or cooperative). For some commodities, such as coffee and cocoa, certification is available only to small-scale producer organisations (cooperatives of small producers): plantations and large family firms cannot generally be certified. Certification is available for large agricultural businesses producing other products such as bananas, tea and fruit, though, where applicable, products must be produced by workers organised in democratically run workers' groups or unions.

The Fair Trade organisations charge certification fees to cooperatives and wholesalers for services such as inspecting the farms and monitoring the supply chain. The minimum charge for certification for the smallest group (fewer than 50 producers) applying for certification of their first product is approximately £1,570 in the first year followed by an annual recertification fee of around £940. The charges for certification of additional products are approximately £165 in the first year followed by an annual recertification fee of £145 (FLO-CERT, 2010). The wholesalers that supply to retailers wishing to use the Fair Trade label also have to pay a licence fee, which is usually based on the wholesale price of the product. For example, in the UK, the Fairtrade Foundation charges 1.7 per cent on the first £5 million of annual sales of Fair Trade certified products and marginally lower for incremental sales thereafter (Fairtrade Foundation, 2010). These fees contribute towards meeting the expenses of the Fair Trade organisations.

Until the late 1990s, Fair Trade products were marketed mainly through Alternative Trade Organisations (ATOs) – traditional outlets such as world shops, NGO charity shops and specialist mail-order companies. The products were mostly procured from producer NGOs in developing countries. The institutional developments in Fair Trade certification and labelling since the 1990s coincide with Fair Trade moving into mainstream marketing and conventional distribution and retail channels. The mainstreaming of Fair Trade proved highly successful, with Fair Trade's profile and sales expanding markedly.

Today, Fair Trade products can be purchased in all major supermarket chains. Supermarket sales have been significantly boosted by the expansion of 'own-brand' Fair Trade labelled products. For example, the UK's Cooperative Group converted all of its own-label coffee and chocolate to Fair Trade in 2002 and 2003 respectively. In December 2006, British retailer Sainsbury's decided to sell only Fair Trade bananas. Many of the large food producers and distributors, such as Procter & Gamble, Nestlé, Kraft, Sara Lee, Chiquita, Del Monte, Dole, Ben and Jerry's, Cadbury (UK and Ireland), Verkade (Netherlands), Toms (Denmark), Candico Sugar, Starbucks and Costa, have also developed Fair Trade lines. According to Rob Cameron, CEO of FLO, 'new brands have embraced Fairtrade and long-standing partners have deepened their commitment. More global brands have made 100 percent commitments than ever before: Cadbury Dairy Milk, Starbucks, Nestlé's Kit Kat, Green & Black's and Ben & Jerry's' (FLO, 2009).

This mainstreaming of Fair Trade has facilitated the extension of the Fair Trade movement beyond traditional products such as coffee, cocoa, tea, handicrafts, honey, preserves and spreads. These new products include minor food items (quinoa), perishable fruits and vegetables (bananas, fruits, vegetables, nuts and seeds and horticultural produce), processed products (juices, wine, beer, chocolate, rice and sugar) and non-food products (cotton).

An important component of the Fair Trade movement is its campaign-based promotion. This is critical for Fair Trade as its growth in sales depends on public awareness and understanding of Fair Trade products and the rationale for buying them.[3] The campaigns range from promoting Fair Trade towns, Fair Trade schools, Fair Trade universities and Fair Trade 'fortnights'; engaging churches, faith groups and media in promoting Fair Trade; specific initiatives for the adoption of Fair Trade purchasing practices by the public sector; and political campaigns and advocacy to change the rules of conventional trade to 'make trade fair'. The campaigning extends to direct participation in mass public protest movements, such as the Jubilee 2000 or Make Poverty History campaigns, debating the links between poverty

---

3   Campaigning is important for Fair Trade – not only for the building of positive attitudes towards it but also for removing scepticism about Fair Trade in the minds of the public (Pelsmacker and Jansens, 2006).

and the perceived injustices of global trade, and arguing for what campaigners describe as trade justice for producers and workers in the global South by 'making trade fair'.

Much of the Fair Trade campaigning work is organised through the Fair Trade networks and the Alternative Trading Organisations (ATOs). For example, Oxfam, UK, one of the pioneering ATOs, focuses on political campaigning and advocacy of Fair Trade. Also, organisations engaged in trading Fair Trade products usually combine trading with Fair Trade campaigning activities. The large-scale retailers and dominant firms engaged in production and in the marketing of Fair Trade lines also promote Fair Trade products and principles. The campaigning reinforces the public legitimacy of the Fair Trade movement, endorsing its definition and inhibiting its dilution into a mere marketing strategy.

Fair Trade: history and institutions

The Fair Trade markets find their roots in more than fifty years of alternative trade relationships. A variety of ATOs proliferated in Europe and North America between the 1950s and 1980s with the objective of helping disadvantaged groups in poor countries.[4] The ATOs working with producer NGOs in developing countries sought to establish trade relations based on principles of trust, charity and solidarity rather than on competition.[5] They began purchasing products, mainly handicrafts, from poor producers or

---

4   The ATOs included Sales Exchange for Refugee Rehabilitation and Vocation (SERRV), Oxfam, Goodwill Selling, Solidaridad, Traidcraft, Christian Aid and other faith and development groups.

5   It should not be thought that 'trust' is not essential to the operation of a competitive market economy!

producer NGOs in the global South at above-market prices, and selling them directly to conscientious consumers in the global North.

In the late 1980s and early 1990s, the ATOs consolidated their efforts within four major associations. The Network of European Worldshops (NEWS!) and the European Fair Trade Association (EFTA[6]) represent national world shop associations and ATOs across Europe. The Fair Trade Federation (FTF) represents ATOs in the USA and Canada as well as producer organisations found largely in Asia. The International Fair Trade Association (IFAT), now called the World Fair Trade Organisation (WFTO), has become the largest umbrella group representing ATOs from Europe (including NEWS! and EFTA), North America and the Pacific, as well as producer organisations and individual members from Latin America, Africa and Asia. These associations act as forums for exchange between producer associations and alternative importers, between marketing organisations and retailers, and also create a web of connections with consumers.

A new dimension was added to the Fair Trade movement with the introduction of the Fair Trade label in 1988. In 1997 the certification and labelling activities of various Fair Trade associations were harmonised and consolidated under the FLO. The FLO represents various Fair Trade national initiatives as well as producer, buyer and consumer groups. Its activities in major markets are overseen by national initiatives such as the TransFair in the USA and the Fairtrade Foundation in the UK. Initially, FLO was both the regulator and provider of certification services. To avoid potential conflicts of interest, an autonomous

6 Confusingly, it has and uses the same initials as the European Free Trade Association.

international inspection and certification company was created from FLO in 2004, the FLO-CERT, which has taken over from FLO the function of providing inspection and certification services among producers, producer groups, exporters and importers. The FLO charges members a Fair Trade certification fee and pays FLO-CERT for its services.

In 1998 the major Fair Trade networks (FLO, IFAT (now WFTO), NEWS! and EFTA) formed an informal alliance called FINE, the name being an acronym created from the first letter of each of the four associations. Its role is to enable these networks and their members to share information and cooperate at strategic levels on crucial issues affecting the future of the Fair Trade movement, such as advocacy, campaigning, standards and monitoring. It maintains a joint Fair Trade Advocacy Office in Brussels, which coordinates the advocacy activities of Fair Trade proponents at the European Union and international levels, as well as building public support for Fair Trade and speaking out on what is described as 'trade justice'.

The evolution of the formal Fair Trade certification and labelling system has enabled the expansion of Fair Trade into mainstream marketing in pursuit of large-volume markets. This has meant Fair Trade entering into business relationships with transnational corporations, large-scale traders, distributors, supermarkets and other retailers. Fair Trade growth is being fuelled by the increasing involvement of mainstream corporate and retail circuits through conventional and costly marketing tools. They now exert greater influence over Fair Trade networks and the product supply chain. Though ATOs played a vital role in shaping and popularising the Fair Trade movement, their role has been somewhat sidelined with the growth of mainstream marketing:

'Fair trade labelling has moved from being a radical solidarity movement to a mainstream trend in retail' (Nicholls and Opal, 2005: 142).

Profile of Fair Trade sales and production

In addition to sales of Fair Trade labelled products, the Fair Trade markets also include ATO products that are sold mainly in ATO world shops and usually include products for which no price structure exists. The same principles of labelled products are adopted in a more flexible spirit for ATO products. Some ATO products involve certification of participatory producer organisations rather than individual products. The labelled product sales data are collected by the FLO and its national affiliates in the certification process and are readily available. There is, however, no uniform or reliable system for compilation of ATO sales figures. They are usually compiled from incomplete surveys or estimated based on assuming ATO world shop sales of 50 per cent labelled and 50 per cent ATO products. According to rough estimates compiled by Raynolds and Long (2007), labelled products accounted for about 88 per cent of the total Fair Trade sales in 2005, the rest being ATO sales. Below, we report only labelled product sales in view of their primacy and the availability and reliability of data.

In 2009 Fair Trade certified sales amounted to approximately €3.4 billion (about £2.8 billion) worldwide, produced by over 1.2 million producers and workers; producers also benefited from pre-financing of around €100 million (£83 million) (FLO, 2009).[7]

---

7   The sales volumes of main Fair Trade certified goods in 2009 (in metric tonnes unless specified otherwise) include: coffee 73,781, bananas 311,465, cocoa 13,898,

The sales represent only around 0.01 per cent of the total food and beverage industry sales worldwide, but what is distinctive is their high growth rate: sales grew by over 40 per cent annually between 1998 and 2007, 22 per cent between 2007 and 2008, and 15 per cent between 2008 and 2009. By the end of 2009 over 27,000 Fair Trade certified products in twenty product groups were available to consumers in over seventy countries (ibid.). Europe and North America are the main markets for Fair Trade products.[8] Fair trade products generally account for 0.5 to 5 per cent of all sales in their product categories in these markets (Raynolds and Long, 2007).

According to FLO (2009), by the end of 2009 a total of 827 producer organisations and roughly 1,170 traders in 60 developing countries were registered with the FLO for supply of Fair Trade certified products (ibid.). Latin America and the Caribbean represent the hub of Fair Trade production. In 2009 Fair Trade producers, workers and their community received total Fair Trade premiums of around €52 million; of these premium payments 65 per cent was used in Latin America and the Caribbean, 24 per cent in Africa and 10 per cent in Asia.

Coffee is the most valuable product within the Fair Trade system. The initial growth of Fair Trade coffee was the result of consumer movements rooted in NGOs and their associated ATOs. In the face of falling coffee prices during the 1980s, the ATOs promoted alternative coffee products designed to embody

---

sugar 89,628, tea 11,524, fresh fruit 20,091, fruit juice 45,582, rice 5,052, honey 2,065, wine about 11 million litres, items made from Fair Trade certified cotton about 23 million pieces (FLO, 2009).

8   The sales of Fair Trade products in the top twelve Fair Trade consuming markets in 2009 (approximate in million euros) include: UK 90; USA 85; France 29; Germany 27; Canada 20; Switzerland 18; Netherlands 9; Finland 9; Sweden 8; Austria 7; Belgium 6 and Denmark 5 (ibid.).

a critique of the imbalance of power in the commodity market and of the growing poverty of coffee farmers, and as part of the wider human rights, anti-poverty, environmental and trade justice movements. The ATO 'Equal Exchange' based in the USA began importing and selling Nicaraguan coffee in support of the Sandinista movement. The Dutch religious organisation 'Solidaridad', working in Mexico, then conceived the idea of a Fair Trade label as a device to distinguish products bought and sold under 'fair trading' conditions. The Max Havelaar Fair Trade label was established to market Mexican and Nicaraguan coffee, which gained a 3 per cent market share in the Netherlands (Webb, 2007).[9]

Since coffee is mostly consumed in the developed world, coffee end products constitute a highly profitable market in the affluent societies of North America, Europe and Australasia. The long-running Fair Trade campaigns succeeded in securing a sizeable market presence for Fair Trade coffee in these markets, and coffee became the dominant product within the Fair Trade movement. In 2007 it accounted for a quarter of Fair Trade sales (FLO, 2007a). With the extension of Fair Trade into new products this share has declined, but coffee still remains the most important Fair Trade product. Although coffee is the Fair Trade product with the highest sales volume, the market share of Fair Trade coffee is estimated at only 1 per cent of worldwide sales of all instant, roast and ground coffee products (Valkila and Nygren, 2009).

The Fair Trade market share of higher-value roast and ground coffee has increased markedly in the UK over the course of the past few years – in 2009 it accounted for 20 per cent of the retail

---

9   The Max Havelaar label certified that a guaranteed minimum price was being paid to the producers, along with additional funds for community development projects.

value of ground coffee. It is also high in some other European countries, with market shares varying between 1 and 7 per cent (Pay, 2009). The high growth in the UK is because of retail growth in the availability of a wide range of coffee drinks through café chains, consumer movements and the establishment of the Fair Trade company Café Direct as a prominent supplier of Fair Trade coffee products. In recent years, the Fair Trade coffee market has increasingly demanded organic coffee. The dual certification of Fair Trade and organic has allowed Fair Trade to differentiate its coffee in a saturated market. The share of organic certified coffee in 2009 was around 40 per cent of total Fair Trade certified coffee (FLO, 2009).

On the one hand, the growth of Fair Trade coffee is evidence of the market impact of alternative trading consumer movements. It is also, on the other hand, perceived as a strategy to increase profitability through creative marketing of products designed to appeal to the consciences of potential consumers.[10] It is argued that the marketing techniques of market segmentation and product differentiation are employed to develop niche markets for Fair Trade coffee. The coffee product market is highly concentrated, with five main coffee processors and roasters (Kraft, Nestlé, Procter & Gamble, Sara Lee and Tchibo) buying approximately half of the global supply of green coffee beans to manufacture coffee end products (Mohan, 2007a). Their adoption of the Fair Trade label for some of their high-value brands has boosted the growth of Fair Trade coffee.

Bananas are now the second most valuable Fair Trade product with sales of around 311,465 million tonnes in 2009 (FLO, 2009),

---

10 Mintel (2006) market research on consumer attitudes shows that an ethical image increases the sales and profitability of a branded product.

though their certification was started only in 1996 in Europe by the Max Havelaar group in association with an importing and distribution company. The sales success can be ascribed to promotion by leading retailers such as Migros, Cooperative and Sainsbury's, some of whom decided to sell only Fair Trade bananas. Fair Trade's entry into bananas (and other fresh produce sectors) has increased the engagement of large enterprises in Fair Trade products. It has required the expansion of Fair Trade certification of large plantations and enterprises, which was earlier done mainly for sugar and tea. The greater scale economies in the production and distribution of fresh produce and their perishability make them more demanding in terms of technical and capital requirements, thus limiting the participation of small-scale enterprises.

Plantations owned by Dole, Chiquita and Del Monte control 40 per cent of production, and a 55–60 per cent market share of the packaging/exporting and importing of bananas supplied to supermarket and independent ripeners/retailers. At times, Fair Trade's engagement with such large plantations is blamed for the erosion of its small farmer base (Raynolds and Long, 2007). Fair Trade's response is that even by engaging with large plantations and enterprises, they are providing support for those workers that labour on Fair Trade certified plantations through better working conditions and the social premium. At the same time, Fair Trade provides new and better markets for relatively smaller enterprises engaged in the market for bananas, thus attempting to provide alternative sales channels in what is a concentrated market with relatively few corporations acting as suppliers (Nicholls and Opal, 2005; Shreck, 2005).

The table below (FLO, 2009) shows the level of and growth in the sales of a sample of main Fair Trade products from 2004 to end 2009.

Table 1 **Growth in sales of some Fair Trade products, 2004–09**

	2004	2005	2006	2007	2008	2009
Coffee sales in metric tonnes	24.22	33.99	52.06	62.21	65.81	73.78
% growth		40.00	53.16	19.49	5.79	12.82
Tea sales in metric tonnes	1.97	1.70	3.88	5.42	11.47	11.52
% growth		33.00	127.88	39.61	111.53	0.50
Rice sales in metric tonnes	1.38	1.70	2.99	4.21	4.69	6.05
% growth		23.00	75.18	40.97	11.34	29.18
Fruit juice sales in metric tonnes	4.54	4.86	6.31	24.92	28.22	45.58
% growth		7.00	23.01	294.98	13.24	61.53
Banana sales in metric tonnes	80.64	103.88	135.76	233.79	299.21	311.47
% growth		29.00	30.70	72.21	27.98	4.10

Source: FLO (2009)

Conclusions

The Fair Trade label shows that the product has been produced and traded according to predefined social, contractual and sometimes environmental standards. Seen in a global context, the sales of Fair Trade products represent only a very small share of products sales worldwide. But what is remarkable is the significant growth in the sales of some Fair Trade products over the past decade, as well as the diversification of Fair Trade into a range of new products. To a large extent this has been fuelled by the engagement of Fair Trade with multinational companies and large corporations. Although this has enabled Fair Trade products to access supermarket shelves with a consequent sharp increase in global sales, it has at the same time diluted the conception of Fair Trade as a component of what some might call the 'solidarity economy' and alternative trading movement, requiring it to work closely with mainstream trading circuits.

2 IS FAIR TRADE FREE MARKET?

Introduction

It is often suggested that Fair Trade is different from free market trade, as if economic thinking has to be left behind when entering the sphere of Fair Trade (Renard, 2003). The proponents of Fair Trade often depict it as an alternative to the hegemony of free trade and an attempt to create alternative distribution channels to combat the structure of world trade, which is regarded as unjust (Brown, 1993). At the same time, critics of Fair Trade often blame it for causing market distortions and overproduction that ultimately works against the interests of those that Fair Trade purports to support.

In this chapter we illustrate that Fair Trade rests as much on market forces as conventional trading does: it is very much a market-responsive model of trade, a consequence of consumer society requiring participants to make a profit. With respect to their substance, Fair Trade and traditionally marketed products show at most very little divergence and hardly differ with respect to their functional utility. They differ merely in terms of following certain production and trading standards that affect the circumstances under which the goods are produced and marketed. This makes Fair Trade very similar to a speciality market operation like that for organic products or local produce. It should be pointed out here that we are simply looking at the facts of how Fair Trade operates in providing goods for consumers. At this stage, we make no comment on the underlying political views of those involved in the Fair Trade movement.

The individual consumer's rational choice

Most economic analyses assume that rational consumers maximise their subjective expected utility, under given constraints, by choosing from a set of available options the alternative that maximises utility. On a priori grounds the behaviour of a Fair Trade consumer deciding in favour of the relatively more expensive Fair Trade product over a relatively similar product that is not Fair Trade seems irrational. Seen from a deeper economic perspective, however, this behaviour is rational because the consumer opts for the relatively expensive Fair Trade product only if the net utility from it is higher than that from a comparable conventional product. This is because the consumers' utility preference function includes a supplementary type of utility in addition to the functional utility from the consumption of the good (Baggini, 2007; Richardson and Stahler, 2007). It is, indeed, only caricatures of the model of market choice which suggest that products are valued for their explicit, quantifiable, material and objective qualities. An Austrian view of the market economy would describe how individuals purposefully pursue objectives known only to them. This may involve the purchase of Fair Trade products because the individual believes that they are doing some good for poor producers, or even the purchase of products because individuals wish to be able to tell other people that they are doing some good. It is only necessary for individuals to *believe* that they are doing something to help others – it is not necessary to assume that consumers do actually assess the evidence.

Even in more classical economic models such a supplementary utility is relevant to consumer decisions. It may develop owing to what Antle (1999) calls 'extrinsic quality'. This is when the consumer wishes to support the producers and workers or cares about the production and the distribution process, even if it does not affect product quality. For some consumers the apparently charitable act of purchasing Fair Trade products may benefit them because they feel they are promoting their social reputation and self-esteem.[1] If the supplementary utility exceeds the utility losses caused by the additional charge for the Fair Trade product compared with the conventional product, then the act of the consumer demanding such a product is fully rational.

Steinrucken and Jaenichen (2007) liken Fair Trade produce to a product bundle.[2] The acquisition of the conventional product is linked to a component that contributes to supplementary utility. For example, Fair Trade coffee is a different product from conventionally traded coffee in terms of attributes that are not necessarily physical in nature: they are more moral or ethical in nature and include circumstances under which the goods are produced and marketed. An alternative for consumers could be to obtain both components separately by buying conventional products and obtaining the supplementary utility by a relevant charitable action or donation to an aid organisation. Nevertheless, it can be argued that the purchase of the product bundle is a rational consumer preference. The preference does not, of course, have to be a *well-informed* choice, but the attraction of buying such a

---

1   Self-esteem is used in the sense of a 'feel good' factor.
2   For the economic theory of product bundling, see Varian (2003).

product bundle could be put down to the fact that the Fair Trade purchase does not cause additional transaction costs for the consumer, such as expense of or time necessary for the collection of information about alternative charitable causes. If the charitable act is bundled with the physical product purchase an individual may find this an efficient way to deliver a small donation.[3]

The Fair Trade product bundle follows a third-degree price discrimination by segmenting consumers between the conventional and the Fair Trade market and preventing transfer of the products between the two markets by the application of the Fair Trade label. Just as conventional products influence consumers through advertising, Fair Trade seeks to influence them through campaigning, in particular telling the consumers that their purchase will help finance a more equitable way of doing business. Whether Fair Trade does or does not achieve its objectives is an empirical matter which has no bearing on the issue of whether it is intrinsically part of the 'free market'. It would seem to satisfy the subjective preferences of consumers, even if those consumers are not perfectly informed. This is not unique to Fair Trade; other alternative models of 'ethical' trading are in many ways quite similar.

The individual producer's rational choice

Some commentators consider the participation of producers in Fair Trade as irrational because it causes market inefficiencies and overproduction, which ultimately works against their own interests. *The Economist* (2006) suggested that by propping

---

3   The lower the costs of moral and ethical behaviour, the higher the willingness to act accordingly (Kirchgässner, 1992; Kirchgässner and Pommerehne, 1993).

up the price, the Fair Trade system could encourage farmers to produce more of the same commodities, rather than diversifying into other crops. This would depress prices, thus achieving, for most farmers, exactly the opposite of what the Fair Trade initiative is intended to do. Leclair (2002), Maseland and de Vaal (2002) and Singleton (2005) make a similar claim: when the price of a commodity, which is traded on world markets, tumbles in response to global oversupply, overcompensated Fair Trade producers will continue production rather than switching to some other product or livelihood. This maintains the oversupply, creating problems for other producers and ultimately Fair Trade producers. In particular, it creates problems for producers who do not have the freedom, or for whom it is more difficult, to switch production. Therefore the supposed benefit to a number of Fair Trade producers from the artificial increase in price is an illusion when seen in the overall context.

There are a number of inconsistencies behind this kind of reasoning. If the minimum price of Fair Trade coffee is set above the market price, as anyone who has taken basic economics would predict, it will lead to an excess supply of Fair Trade coffee, but it does little to increase general coffee production. The increase in the supply of Fair Trade coffee is from the channelling of existing production into the Fair Trade market, not by inducing producers in general to grow more coffee – the price of non-Fair Trade coffee may fall if this effect is significant. Fair Trade producers are fully aware that they are able to sell only a small share of their produce in the Fair Trade market and the rest of their produce they still have to sell in the conventional market.

The share of coffee a certified small producer can sell through Fair Trade channels is often only 30 per cent; the rest has to be sold on the conventional market without any premium (Kohler, 2006). Fair Trade cocoa producers in Ghana could sell only 8 per cent of their crop to Fair Trade and Fair Trade coffee producers in Tanzania sold only 10 per cent (Riedel et al., 2005) – though these figures may well have increased since Fair Trade became mainstream. On average, Mexican Fair Trade certified cooperatives sell only 20 per cent of their production in the Fair Trade market (Renard and Grovas, 2007). Owing to limited demand, many Fair Trade certified cooperatives in northern Nicaragua sell close to 70 per cent of their coffee into the conventional markets (Bacon, 2005).

The excess supply of Fair Trade certified coffee therefore does not cause large quantities of coffee to be dumped on world markets. It represents only a reallocation of resources based on competitive supply and demand, and there are no grounds for any claim that Fair Trade distorts competition and promotes inefficiency (Hayes, 2006). 'Fair Trade cannot be expected to fix the basic problem afflicting many commodity markets. If there is an excessive production of coffee, the reasons lie elsewhere; Fair Trade coffee is not changing the demand for coffee as it does not affect the complex conditions that determine coffee prices in different markets' (FLO, 2007b). As would be expected, if supply exceeds demand in Fair Trade markets this results in increased barriers to entry and increased competition among Fair Trade producers and producer organisations for the limited number of Fair Trade contracts.

There are, of course, barriers to entry for Fair Trade producers. There is a selection process carried out by buyers who enjoy market power to discriminate between different suppliers. For example, if a new producer wishes to sell Fair Trade, it is required first to find a buyer for the product. Fair Trade organisations then charge traders, wholesalers and producer organisations for Fair Trade certification (see Chapter 1). Therefore, from an economic point of view, barriers to entering the Fair Trade market have intensified to equilibrate supply and demand in a market with a price floor. In practice, there has been a continual rise in the quality of the product demanded by buyers from the suppliers of Fair Trade products since 2000. This emphasis has limited the participation of some producers and favoured commercially oriented suppliers able to provide the required product quality (Wilkinson, 2007).[4] An example is the Fair Trade coffee market demanding organic coffee so that producers and producer organisations increasingly find that, despite the cost, they also have to become organic certified to obtain Fair Trade contracts.[5]

When it comes to producers deciding whether to join Fair Trade, they do so by comparing the demands or costs imposed by Fair Trade with the expected pay-offs. They will join only if they expect the pay-offs to be greater than the costs. It is possible that for some producers and for some regions adjusting production according to Fair Trade standards may incur no great additional costs: Fair Trade activities are likely to favour such producers and regions. Some producers may join Fair Trade as a result of considerations such as location of production, quality of output,

---

4   This is also demonstrated by studies on coffee growers in Mexico, quinoa growers in Bolivia and the Brazilian orange juice sector (Raynolds and Murray, 2007).

5   Most organic certification programmes usually require an annual external inspection from the certifying entity, which for an organisation of 100 producers can generally cost around $2,000. The more significant cost, however, is in organising organic production among participating producers. The total cost of implementing an organic certification programme in four Peruvian coffee organisations ranged from $300 to more than $1,000 per producer (Weber, 2006).

diversification of markets or because they are less competitive in conventional markets. In economic terms, producers see Fair Trade as another channel through which to sell their produce, and will defect from Fair Trade if they feel the pay-offs are not to their advantage. Therefore it is a rational free market decision from the viewpoint of producers to produce for Fair Trade, and doing so cannot be blamed for causing market distortion or overproduction.

It could be argued (though we do not argue here) that the requirement for Fair Trade producers to follow certain standards provides them with little net benefit after allowing for the costs. It can also be argued that the benefits to the producer are not what the consumer might suppose. But this is true with many types of market trade (for example, organic and local produce). It is also true that consumers receive subjective benefits from consuming all types of products in a market economy, and that those subjective benefits may be difficult to justify objectively. In all these circumstances, producers have to 'jump through hoops' to satisfy consumers. In no sense does the fact that Fair Trade producers have to satisfy certain conditions make Fair Trade not part of the free economy. Whether Fair Trade helps the people it claims to help is an entirely different question.

Fair Trade: an alternative speciality market distribution channel

Essentially, Fair Trade is an alternative form of speciality trade that is sending a market signal. Fair Trade prices are not stopping any free market price signals, they are just communicating the price for an additional bundle of subjective services for which, it appears, consumers are willing to pay. Fair Trade provides an additional trade channel that, among other things, offers opportunities to particular consumers to obtain supplementary utility and to certain producers to access an additional marketing channel that offers possibilities to capture a price premium.

Just as an organic speciality market supplier can earn more compared with a 'mainstream' supplier, the same holds for a Fair Trade supplier. They can benefit, however, only to the extent of the size of the Fair Trade speciality market. Fair Trade sellers have to rely on developing their own brand recognition, knowing that their products face aware and discerning free market buyers who have wide choices. Since the early days of Fair Trade most sellers have been aware that customer loyalty for Fair Trade products hinges on their quality and price in relation to competing brands. Fair Trade consumers are happy to pay extra for conscience-soothing coffee today, but will not continue to do so for ever if the quality of the coffee does not match that of competing brands (Howley, 2006).

Becchetti and Rosati (2007) and Hiscox (2007) support the alternative speciality market argument. The food industry produces highly differentiated products with a continuous wave of innovations that create new varieties. There is not one single coffee but instead many different coffee products which are differentiated from one another in terms of quality, blends, packaging and also, more recently, 'social responsibility' features. For each of these products there exists a specific and different market price which is determined by consumer taste for that kind of product. For instance, the Fair Trade coffee market is a different market from the mainstream coffee market. The different sub-markets have different supply and demand curves based on the choices of consumers and producers. The specialised brands can create more inelastic demand by segmenting the market. If the market for Fair Trade coffee supports a higher price, the signal this sends is that coffee producers should compete to capture a part of this higher price. All the costs associated with producing Fair Trade coffee are priced in the Fair Trade coffee market, and consumers voluntarily pay this price by purchasing this coffee.

From the point of view of economic theory, there are several different market niches, just one of which is Fair Trade. Like the market for organic food or for kosher meat, Fair Trade products have particular attributes in addition to the physical nature of the product and have their own market equilibrium. Consumers of Fair Trade products form a kind of speciality market club, which can be joined voluntarily by those who are willing to pay extra for the Fair Trade product bundle. These people signal their willingness to pay a premium and economic agents in the supply chain, including producers, respond to these signals. This is no different from some other speciality market operations. For example, in the case of coffee the trading networks of Fair Trade, organic, shade-grown or single-origin coffee have acted to distinguish their alternative product qualities through certification designed to symbolise social solidarity, ecology, flavour or regional identity (Renard, 1999; Weber, 2007).

Fair Trade mainstreaming

The mainstreaming of the Fair Trade movement has extended its scope and size.[6] The participation of ATOs continues, though they

---

6   For example, the use by transnationals such as Cadbury of Fair Trade chocolate or the sale of Fair Trade bananas as the only type available in some leading supermarkets.

are exposed to a greater degree of competition from other market players. Some of them have adjusted to this by professionalising their staff and relocating their shops. Some ATOs have directed their attention to mobilising support from the public sector to obtain recognition and preferences for public procurement supplies. The disadvantages and advantages of mainstreaming are widely debated in the Fair Trade literature.

Many feel that it creates contradictions with the Fair Trade movement's philosophical foundations, which are built on an alternative consumer–producer relationship. There is a fear that mainstreaming would result in the movement being overtaken by the strategies of mainstream companies, eroding the movement's capacity to help marginalised producers and workers through an alternative trading system. This mainstreaming might contradict the movement's historical charter of challenging what it regards as the unjust and inequitable nature of conventional international trade. They feel that it would ultimately result in the movement maturing into a less dynamic phenomenon than it was before the onset of mainstreaming (Marsden et al., 2000; Raynolds, 2002; Renard, 2003; Wilkinson and Mascarenhas, 2007).

Others consider mainstreaming to be in the best interests of the movement. Without mainstreaming, the movement will remain a fringe market ATO operation that supports a few privileged groups. ATOs played a vital role in shaping the movement, but there is a clear limit to their direct sales strategy – and therefore a limit to the number of producers who can benefit. The enlisting of the resources of mainstream retailers has put Fair Trade in the forefront in terms both of higher sales and of a higher number of products sold under the banner of Fair Trade. Mainstreaming expands awareness for Fair Trade products and principles; it reinforces Fair Trade campaigns; raises the public demand for its products (Tallontire and Vorley, 2005); and also means that consumers can choose between a wide range of brands offered by a large number of sellers while still remaining loyal to Fair Trade.

Regardless, the growth of mainstreaming requires the Fair Trade networks to work with conventional commodity chains and with both large and small-scale producers and traders, while at the same time maintaining the speciality market characteristics. This does pose a challenge for the Fair Trade movement and institutions as they need to be able to adapt to the sourcing, branding, packaging and other market demands of conventional mainstream trading circuits without an erosion of their traditional principles: in particular the ability to benefit smallholder producers.

Conclusion

It is wrong to consider Fair Trade as a development of a market that is different from the 'free market'. All that is happening is that Fair Trade opens up an alternative speciality trading channel within the free market. The market fundamentals, the demand, supply and market competitiveness conditions for Fair Trade products, follow conventional trade practices. Fair Trade works not because it subsidises goods no one wants, but because some free market consumers are willing to support it. Whether they are 'objectively' right to do so is important but irrelevant to this particular line of argument[7] – Fair Trade fulfils a subjective

---

7   Certainly in the eyes of free market Austrian economists.

preference. Fair Trade products have to compete in the market just like any other speciality market product. Fair Trade producers can receive the Fair Trade prices and premiums only if they have a buyer willing to pay them. Therefore Fair Trade does not pose a challenge to the free market system; rather it is a part of that system that increases the welfare of a target group through a speciality market. Whether Fair Trade provides the benefits to the producers that the buyers believe or imposes costs on others who are less fortunate are separate but important issues.

3 BENEFITS AND DETRIMENTS OF FAIR TRADE

Introduction

Fair Trade imposes certain conditions and costs on Fair Trade producers and traders, and its campaigning tells consumers what is good or bad. The campaigning tends to convey the idea that Fair Trade is 'equitable' while conventional trade is based on exploitation, causing hardships to commodity producers and workers in the developing world. This is reflected in the FINE's listing of the goals of Fair Trade, which include the following:

- raising awareness among consumers of the negative effects on producers of international trade so that they exercise their purchasing power positively;
- campaigning for changes in the rules and practice of conventional international trade.

This draws reaction from commentators and makes Fair Trade controversial.

Some commentators (Potts, 2004; Sellers, 2005; Jacquiau, 2006; Howley, 2006; Booth and Whetstone, 2007; Weber, 2007; Henderson, 2008) feel that Fair Trade faces serious practical issues and that a large gap divides the purported benefits depicted by Fair Trade promotional materials and the reality or advantages of producer participation in Fair Trade. Those commentators argue that it is wrong to convey the idea that products without the Fair Trade label are based on unfair treatment and penalise producers and marketers. The Fair Trade rhetoric undermines and distracts attention from the development opportunities that conventional international trade offers producers and workers in developing nations. It also seems to ignore the huge growth in incomes that has arisen as a result of conventional trade in countries that adopt the right conditions for development. Therefore, as the visibility of Fair Trade has grown over the years, so has the criticism and scepticism surrounding it. This chapter evaluates the evidence on the benefits and misgivings surrounding Fair Trade.

Benefits of Fair Trade
A guaranteed minimum 'fair' price and a social premium

The FINE states that certified Fair Trade benefits marginalised producers and workers in developing countries by providing them with guaranteed minimum prices that may be higher than conventional world market prices; it also provides a social premium to finance wider community projects such as health clinics, schools, roads, sanitation and other social services. According to the FLO (2009) estimates, in 2009 around €52 million (US$65 million) was provided as a social premium to Fair Trade producers and their communities above and beyond the Fair Trade price. This money helps to build Fair Trade producers' and workers' communities through, for example, providing access to clean water, the ability to purchase household implements, the support of transportation and community infrastructure and the education of producers' children.

TransFair in the USA campaigns for Fair Trade saying: 'the best way to give small-scale producers in developing countries a real opportunity towards a better life is to give them a fair chance to produce and market their products'. The Fairtrade Foundation, the UK's Fair Trade standards agency, advocates the message: 'Fair Trade offers a chance for farmers and workers to increase their control over their own future, have a fair and just return for work, have continuity of income and decent working and living conditions through sustainable development.'

These expressions by the Fair Trade organisations are endorsed by other commentators. For small-scale producers, the most direct benefits from Fair Trade come from higher guaranteed prices and the social premium which is supposed to be invested in production facilities and community projects. For larger enterprises the price floor helps provide economic stability, and the social premium is intended to enhance worker welfare through investments in training, equipment, ownership shares and broader community welfare through the provision of various social services (Grodnik and Conroy, 2007). The guaranteed Fair Trade price also insures risk-averse primary product producers against the variability of market prices, particularly in tropical commodity markets that face high levels of price fluctuations. For example, Fair Trade coffee seeks to counter falling producer prices, international market volatility and the vulnerability of small-scale producers (Bacon, 2005; Grodnik and Conroy, 2007). Therefore, through the use of a voluntary price floor, Fair Trade, in effect, operates as a very simple hedging device for small farmers, rather like a 'put option' in a sales contract (Berndt, 2007).

Organisational capacity-building

It is also argued that Fair Trade certification empowers farmers and farm workers to lift themselves out of poverty. It is an approach to trade that has a strong development rationale, based on introducing previously excluded producers to potentially lucrative niche markets and providing access to pre-finance. Regardless of the cause of producers in poor countries being excluded from trade finance and lucrative markets in developed countries – arguably it is poor governance in underdeveloped countries – it can be argued that Fair Trade does provide these important economic benefits. Fair Trade may also help producers and workers by supporting organisational capacity-building for the democratic groups that are required to represent small-scale producers (via cooperatives) and workers (via unions). In so doing, Fair Trade enhances production and marketing skills for participants and their families which extend beyond Fair Trade production into civil society more widely.

Fair Trade claims to support marginalised producers of coffee and cocoa by giving them more control over their selling operation by requiring them to belong to producer cooperatives, thereby reducing the need for them to sell to (sometimes unscrupulous) middlemen (called 'coyotes'). Furthermore, cooperatives allow producers to take advantage of economies of scale to bargain more effectively with large buyers of products; good cooperatives help by creating business plans, negotiating credit and providing credit to members, providing training in organic farming techniques and organising organic certification, improving quality control and building relations with foreign importers. Boudreaux's (2007) study of selected cooperatives in Rwanda reports that Fair Trade institutions helped teach members how to improve their quality

control, develop effective marketing strategies, and create beneficial relationships with speciality coffee importers, though a large
part of the success can be attributed to the PEARL project that
helps promote speciality coffee.

Tallontire et al. (2001) argue that engagement in Fair Trade
also provides a stimulus for producers and workers to reorganise
their production processes in a socially and environmentally more
acceptable manner. Field studies by Bacon (2005), Boot et al.
(2003), Murray et al. (2003), Nelson et al. (2002) and Zadek and
Tiffin (1996), assessing the local impact of Fair Trade certification
in producing countries, suggest that it has in general been beneficial for producers in the development of their organisational
skills.

A more equitable trading partnership

Fair Trade networks seek to reform international commodity
exchange by establishing new forms of exchange between
Southern producers and Northern consumers, as expressed
through social arrangements based on solidarity and coordinated
action, by connecting them through international trade networks
dedicated to producers and their communities. The empower-
ment that results from this is not simply a function of increased
incomes but rests on long-term benefits that can potentially help
producers, producer organisations and workers in developing
countries (Raynolds et al., 2004; Lockie, 2006; FLO, 2007a).

Raynolds (2002), Ransom (2005), Berndt (2007) and
Goodman (2007) endorse this, arguing that Fair Trade seeks
to redirect globalisation's transformative powers towards the
creation of greater equity in international trade and social equity

on a global scale. The Fair Trade movement critiques conventional production, trade and consumption relations and seeks to create new and more egalitarian commodity networks linking consumers in the global North with marginalised producers in the global South, empowering the latter to become stakeholders in their own organisations and actively play a wider role in the global arena, to achieve greater equity in international trade.

It is not necessary to accept this analysis of Fair Trade – which implies a strong criticism of free trade and globalisation that is often characteristic of Fair Trade's proponents – to agree that benefits arise from Fair Trade. A different line of argument could accept that producers in the South were excluded from many of the benefits of globalisation as a result of the absence of the necessary conditions for development within many countries that produce primary products. Fair Trade, it could be argued, provides a different set of market-institutional arrangements that is suited to the needs of such primary product producers. It does so by creating more competition in the markets for primary products, as well as assisting with trade credit and the building of organisational capacity.

The gap: promotional claims and reality
Fair Trade and the actual transfer to producers

Fair Trade's proponents try to convey the impression that almost all the price premium they are paying for Fair Trade products is passed on to the producer, while the reality is very different (Potts, 2004; Harford, 2005; Sellers, 2005; Weber, 2007). Jacquiau (2006) is concerned with the question of how much of the money spent on Fair Trade products actually ends up in the pockets of producers in developing countries; it seems that they generally receive only a small fraction of the extra margin consumers pay: perhaps as little as 10 per cent of the additional price paid for Fair Trade coffee trickles down to the producer. Even analysts who are sympathetic to Fair Trade (such as Nicholls and Opal, 2005) estimate that, at the most, only 25 per cent of the additional price a shopper pays for Fair Trade bananas would go to the producers, largely because wholesalers (including producer organisations), traders (importers) and retailers all increase their mark-ups. According to Nicholls and Opal, the mark-ups are mainly to cover the Fair Trade certification fees that wholesalers and traders pay to the Fair Trade organisations and to offset the costs incurred in organising the additional supply chains and marketing channels for Fair Trade products.

The Fair Trade certification fees are criticised for being excessive. Howley (2006), Booth and Whetstone (2007) and Henderson (2008) are critical of the administration and promotional costs of Fair Trade. They feel that Fair Trade has grown into a complex bureaucracy and an industry in itself. Consequently, it has to charge high certification fees to cover these costs, which eats up a major proportion of the Fair Trade price premium. The Fair Trade viewpoint is that it needs to have in place proper systems of checking and conducting inspections all through the supply chain – something which is expensive. The high expenditure on promotional activities is necessary as Fair Trade's success depends upon reaching consumers and building their capacity to pay a premium for its products: Fair Trade can exist as long as some consumers' willingness to pay is sufficient to cover the costs of the Fair Trade process.

There are also concerns that wholesalers, processors, branders and retailers add their own mark-ups to Fair Trade products to identify price-insensitive consumers who are willing to pay more. Fair Trade's consumers are likely to be price inelastic. As such, part of the premium is extra profit for those in the later parts of the supply chain. Fair Trade has no control over those extra dips into the profit chain (Economist, 2006). According to *Financial Times* writer Harford (2005), for several years only 10 per cent of the premium that Costa, a UK coffee bar, charged for Fair Trade coffee reached the producer. The other 90 per cent went to Costa's bottom line. So why was Costa charging so much more? Perhaps Fair Trade coffee 'allowed Costa to find customers who are willing to pay a bit more if given a reason to do so'.[1]

The UK Fairtrade Foundation's (2006) response to this is that Fair Trade works in the way the free enterprise system works – it merely guarantees that a fair price is paid to the producer, and has no way of controlling margins in the rest of the supply chain. Moreover, under EU and US competition laws, it is illegal for Fair Trade to intervene in price-fixing discussions between retailers and importers. The Foundation cites a range of studies conducted in 2005 to show that the majority of retailers do not increase their profit margins on Fair Trade products for fear of losing their market share in the growing Fair Trade market. Also, retailers are not likely to misuse Fair Trade as they are now increasingly concerned about image improvement and wish to be seen doing something to help poor producers. In December 2006, for example, British retailer Sainsbury's announced that it would offer only Fair Trade bananas – and this was achieved without any increase in the cost paid by consumers.

---

1   Costa stopped charging the extra amount when the anomaly was pointed out to them.

Notwithstanding whether the costs of organising and managing the Fair Trade process are justified or not, there is no denying the fact that a major proportion of the gain from the Fair Trade price premium is eaten up in the supply chain and, to that extent, the premium available for redistribution to producers is reduced. In addition, producers are likely to incur additional expenditure in meeting the Fair Trade certification standards. Therefore, despite the Fair Trade scheme making an explicit provision for a price premium, the net premium actually received by producers can be far lower than is commonly perceived.[2] It may be worth noting that it is wrong to assume that producers join Fair Trade only for the premium; as noted earlier, there can be other reasons, such as lack of access to other marketing institutions or a wish to diversify their marketing options.

Does Fair Trade secure producers against the volatility of market prices?

The Fair Trade contract involves fixing a minimum guaranteed price to be received by producers regardless of supply and demand conditions at the time the product is delivered. A literal interpretation of this contract condition has resulted in the propagation of the claim that Fair Trade insures producers against the variability of market prices. The claim runs into problems, however. This is because producers are not concerned with price per se, but price is important to them to the extent that it affects their income (Mohan and Love, 2004). The guaranteed price can guarantee income only if there is also a guarantee of the quantities

---

2   The premium received could still be attractive for some producers, particularly smallholders, when seen in relation to their very low average incomes.

that traders will buy from them. It is not possible for Fair Trade to guarantee the quantities that will be bought at the guaranteed price, as importers have to sell Fair Trade products under their own brands and will buy at the guaranteed price only the amount that the market demands; in poor market conditions this demand can fall.[3] Therefore, the guaranteed price without guaranteed quantities does not provide a guaranteed income. The normal uncertainties that surround investment and production planning for primary producers remain. In other words, the guaranteed price cannot serve the purpose of a simple income-hedging device for a producer without a performance (counterparty) guarantee for quantity to cover for default on the part of the buyer.

In fairness to Fair Trade, it does encourage buyers to purchase from producers or producer organisations using agreements that extend preferably beyond a single production (harvest) cycle. One can expect such agreements, when they exist, to ensure a stable income flow. Even if there is an agreement, however, producers may not be in a position to enforce it given that, for most products, the balance of power usually favours the buyers. For example, in coffee markets the dominance of buyers is evident: it is not unheard of for Fair Trade producers to be afraid to ask for pre-financing because buyers have threatened to terminate the partnership; and there are reports that Fair Trade producers are increasingly expected to acquire costly organic certification at the request of buyers or else they have to exit from Fair Trade (Kohler, 2006; Wilkinson and Mascarenhas, 2007). Also, there is no official mechanism for enforcing the agreement: a trader cannot

---

3   Similarly, a producer is not bound to supply; hence, the Fair Trade scheme in-
     volves no binding on either side. The Fair Trade partnership is therefore vulner-
     able to market forces (Hayes, 2006).

be sanctioned for switching from one producer to other. Besides, if buyers so desire, it is easy enough for them to find excuses for not honouring their purchase commitments.

Moreover, commodity markets are notorious for their complexities, which can cause prices to fluctuate widely. If this adversely affects Fair Trade buyers, even well-intentioned buyers will find it difficult to keep their commitments. Some commercial buyers of commodities, including transnational export firms, do guarantee prices to suppliers in order to bring stability to the supply chain, but they do so only after hedging their risk in the commodity derivative market. For example, grain elevator operators in the USA are able to offer pre-announced minimum prices for assured quantities to their suppliers, but only after hedging against market instabilities through forward and futures contracts (Mohan, 2007a). The sort of guarantees that Fair Trade claim are provided to producers are therefore not as secure as might be thought by many purchasers. Furthermore, useful guarantees might be available in other ways.

Nevertheless, Fair Trade is responsible for the creation of an additional trade channel. Studies show, and a priori reasoning tells us, that participation in any form of alternative trade network serves the purpose of diversification, which reduces exposure and vulnerability to low and variable prices. This is endorsed, among others, by Bacon's (2005) findings on organic and speciality coffee producers in northern Nicaragua. Admittedly, Fair Trade deserves credit for this as well as for promoting an institutional purchase agreement, but its campaigners cannot trumpet that it is offering developing-country producers a stable price that secures them against market vulnerabilities. Such a claim borders on overenthusiasm because Fair Trade cannot truly guarantee the quantities that a buyer will purchase from a producer. There is certainly no guaranteed income for Fair Trade producers.

Does Fair Trade challenge unequal trading relationships?

One of the explicit goals of Fair Trade advocates is to correct market distortions and the establishment of equitable trade relations with the South. Several arguments have been advanced in support of this: Fair Trade seeks to challenge market competitiveness based solely on price and campaigns for changes to conventional trade rules and practices. Fair Trade is an innovative concept that connects producers and consumers in more equitable, more meaningful and more sustainable ways (Trans-Fair USA, 2002; Murray and Raynolds, 2007). These arguments have drawn strong reactions from a large number of analysts and commentators, who dismiss them as nothing but rhetoric. One does not have to be a trade protectionist or accept Marxist models of development and trade, however, to see some logic in the Fair Trade arguments – even if the rhetoric they use to justify their arguments is out of place. It is quite possible that, in very poor countries, where business opportunities are limited because the basic prerequisites for the development of a market economy do not exist, primary product producers will be in a situation that exposes them to the market power of buyers. Alternatively – or additionally – such producers may be trapped in low-income activities because the natural market processes by which they would move into more lucrative activities are inhibited by their governments. Finally, trade restrictions in the West on certain primary products and basic manufactured foods might reduce the world price of products and prevent migration up the value chain.

Fair Trade might provide an opportunity for primary product producers in these situations to obtain better prices and higher incomes, but whether it does so in practice is an empirical matter.

The Fair Trade model proposes trade that is as direct as possible, eliminating unnecessary 'middlemen' between importers and producers. But the capacity of Fair Trade to reduce the number of intermediaries is questionable. Local intermediaries have been the traditional means of access for most small producers, and for many Fair Trade producers these have been replaced by producer organisations. At times, Fair Trade production on the ground is much more complex than conventional production in that firms are often required to ensure supply of a particular desired quality and quantity. Moreover, it is wrong to assume that trading in conventional commodity markets entails a large number of intermediaries. Many of the products traded in these markets have witnessed a reduction in the number of intermediaries in the product supply chain with improved communication, transportation and growing vertical integration (Krivonos, 2004; Mohan and Russell, 2008). When it comes to large commercially oriented producers, they enjoy direct market access with or without Fair Trade. Therefore it is difficult to conclusively say that Fair Trade is more direct than conventional trade.

We noted earlier that the market competitiveness conditions for Fair Trade products follow conventional trade practices. Fair Trade cannot change the underlying demand and supply conditions in the product supply chain. For example, in the coffee chain, the structural demand and supply mismatch provides considerable power to traders and roasters, a situation that cannot be addressed by Fair Trade. If the costs and profits are concentrated at the upper end of the supply chain, this is not altered by Fair Trade. Largely, it is a reflection of the productivity of labour and capital in developed countries. Barriers to entry tend to restrict the Fair Trade market to a few already established producers and producer organisations, leaving many out of the Fair Trade system (Weber, 2007). Fair Trade can do no more than enlarge the total income size of the supply chain by means of asking a price premium from consumers, a part of which goes towards meeting the Fair Trade standards with the rest shared in the supply chain, including payment of a fair price to producers (Mendoza and Bastiaensen, 2003; Murdian and Pelupessy, 2005).

It is true that producers of commodities such as coffee, cocoa, tea and bananas have been adversely affected by long periods of decline in prices. It is wrong, however, to blame international trading systems for this. The reasons for this have been well researched in the economics literature. On the demand side, these commodities have low income elasticities of demand so that, as income rises, the share of income spent on them decreases. On the supply side, developing countries faced with acute foreign exchange shortages have tended to expand their commodity exports through increases in government subsidies and support in order to increase export earnings. When this is done by a number of developing countries simultaneously, the resulting expansion of exports only adds to the downward pressure on commodity prices. Low commodity prices can continue over a long period because of the high initial sunk costs involved in production planning so that producers do not exit for want of any other attractive alternatives (Maizels et al., 1997; Mohan, 2005).[4] There-

---

4   It may be pertinent to mention that the fall in commodity prices does not neces-
    sarily imply an equivalent fall in the real income of commodity producers. This
    is because a part of the price decline for many commodities is explained by the

fore, the low coffee prices in the world markets are mainly because of structural demand and supply imbalance, and it is wrong to blame market exploitation by high-end importers, roasters and marketers for it.

When it comes to Fair Trade connecting consumers and producers, consumers see Fair Trade as a social movement, feeling they are establishing relationships with the suppliers of their 'staple' products, whereas most producers tend simply to consider it as another marketing channel. Lyon's (2007) research on a coffee cooperative in Guatemala found that only three of the 53 surveyed members (coffee producers) were familiar with the words 'Fair Trade'. Fair Trade remains an abstract concept for many of them, and few see themselves as part of a broader movement engaging Northern consumers. They see it as just another avenue to sell their produce, and will defect from Fair Trade as soon as a small price advantage is identified (Murray et al., 2006). Research in diverse locales indicates that producers understand Fair Trade in terms of market access and not as an equitable trade relationship in which they are actively participating (Lyon, 2007).

Some criticisms of Fair Trade

Fair Trade is often criticised for being exclusive, unrealistic in its expectations of suppliers and imposed by stronger stakeholders (Farnworth and Goodman, 2006). It is seen to reflect the values of Northern consumers, activists and NGOs, with limited participation of Southern producers. It is also argued that under the Fair Trade scheme transparency occurs mostly at the producer end of

decline in unit cost as a result of supply expansion from rising productivity.

the supply chain, while there is much less information disclosure from and inspection of economic agents in the rest of the supply chain (Wilkinson, 2007). We now move on to discuss various criticisms of Fair Trade.

Fair Trade is exclusive and damages other suppliers

Some commentators question the capability of Fair Trade to target marginalised producers, given complex entry requirements and growing competition in Fair Trade markets. Procedures such as the necessity to join or form an effective producer organisation in the case of coffee and cocoa producers mean that Fair Trade requires substantial initiative and basic capacities and capabilities, which exclude some producers from participating (Lyon, 2006; Weber, 2007). For example, entering the Fair Trade coffee market, especially the Fair Trade organic market, presents major difficulties for producers with limited resources.

Many authors[5] have pointed out that certified Fair Trade products tend to be produced mainly in South and Central America – this is especially true with coffee, though it is quite contrary to the impression often given by those marketing Fair Trade. This raises two issues. The first is whether Fair Trade, by raising the attractiveness of primary product production in the relatively rich countries on which it focuses, raises world supply and thus makes life more difficult for farmers in poorer countries (or for those who do not have the capacity or appropriate business model to become Fair Trade). It is difficult to deny that this is a theoretical problem. Problems of this sort created by Fair

---

5   For example, Sidwell (2007) and Griffiths (2010).

Trade, however, are unlikely to be substantial *as long as Fair Trade remains a relatively small player in the market as a whole.* Paradoxically, insofar as Fair Trade is successful in its mission, it might help undermine the position of the very poorest farmers. There is no evidence to suggest that this is a problem thus far. Also, Smith (2009) has emphasised that Fair Trade focuses on relatively developed but highly unequal societies. He claims that many of the farmers operating as Fair Trade producers in Mexico are some of the poorest in the world because of the high inequality present in Mexico's economy. He argues that case studies conducted in areas such as Mexico's Chiapas region support these views. These studies show considerable improvements in income and conditions for Mexican Fair Trade producers.

Collier (2007) has also argued that the improved trading conditions that arise as a result of Fair Trade might keep farmers working in an industry that should be allowed to decline. Again, this is a theoretical possibility, the practical implications of which are likely to be greater the more successful Fair Trade is. There is no real evidence, however, that development is impeded by Fair Trade in this way, though we do argue below that Fair Trade is not a route to general long-term development as such.

Despite these counter-arguments, it is likely to be the case that Fair Trade consumers do not realise that the focus of Fair Trade is on middle-income rather than on lower-income countries. The top four nations by Fair Trade certified producers,[6] in 2007 were Mexico, Colombia, Peru and South Africa.[7] These nations had an

---

6   Data sourced from FLO (2007a).
7   With thanks to IEA intern and UCLA student Paul Stoddart for the analysis in this paragraph.

TRADE

DP per capita of $4,790[8] in 2007. The thirteen nations with only one Fair Trade certified producer had average GDP per capita of just $2,807 in 2007. Coffee-producing countries with no Fair Trade producers have an even lower average GDP per head. These data are not particularly helpful, however, as they do not indicate the share of Fair Trade in total production in different countries. Of more interest is the relationship between the share of Fair Trade coffee exports of total coffee exports (a measure of Fair Trade penetration) and national income per head and/or poverty. Using data from 2005–07 for Fair Trade exports to the USA,[9] it is not possible to find any significant negative relationship between national income per head or poverty and Fair Trade penetration. Indeed, the relationships that were found (though statistically insignificant) suggest that Fair Trade penetration is greater where income per head is greater; that penetration is greater the more equal is the distribution of incomes; and that penetration is greater the stronger the rule of law. This is a challenge for the Fair Trade organisations which claim that Fair Trade provides development opportunities for producers in very poor countries – the reality is that it may be diverting at least some demand from poor to better-off countries whose producers have a better capacity to organise and pay the relevant fees.

Fair Trade's requirements are damaging

Fair Trade is ultimately driven by the demands of Western consumers. It is not the benefits that accrue to poor producers

---

8 Own calculation based on data from the ERS International Macroeconomic Data Set.

9 There is insufficient data available for other countries.

which determine the premium consumers are willing to pay, but the outcomes that Western consumers believe to be good for poor producers. For example, certified Fair Trade restricts casual labour and prohibits child labour. Much has been written about the problems of restricting child labour in very poor countries. On the whole, poor families do not send their children to work to be cruel to them but to help provide a basic income for the family.[10] A prohibition on child labour may be damaging for families – and also for children who may be forced into other dangerous occupations. The Fairtrade Foundation would argue that the social premium ensures that children should be able to attend school instead of working. The fact of the prohibition on child labour remains, however. It would be better if these problems were managed by poor families themselves rather than by impositions of Western consumers thousands of miles away from the problem of dire child poverty.

Similar arguments can be made regarding Fair Trade's environmental requirements. To what extent do these reflect Westerners' values rather than the realities of trading out of poverty? Haight and Henderson (2010) strongly criticise the prohibition on genetically modified (GM) crops, which they argue is potentially damaging – especially in the banana trade. Again, it should be asked whether this requirement is really designed to satisfy Western consumers' own views about how other people should farm rather than to meet the real needs of very poor farmers. As Haight and Henderson point out, bananas are sterile and prone to disease. GM technology might be the most effective way of producing more reliable banana crops. The Fairtrade Labelling

---

10   The evidence is very strong on this point, and as incomes rise, child labour reduces.

Organization states: 'FLO believes GMO crops are incompatible with Fairtrade.'[11] It is extremely difficult to justify that statement.

As well as concerns over the standards that are imposed, concerns have been expressed about whether those standards are actually met in practice or whether they are meaningful. In many respects the requirements for the treatment of labour simply replicate industry norms, international standards and the countries' own regulations (see ibid.). The only benefit Fair Trade could bring, where this is the case, is that of more active inspection and enforcement. There is no evidence that this is taking place. Weitzman (2006) found that four out of five Fair Trade coffee suppliers to a cooperative in Peru paid less than the legal minimum wage to workers, and such payments do not violate Fair Trade standards. Fair Trade promotional materials, however, have lured coffee drinkers into believing that Fair Trade guarantees farmers and workers a fair or living wage, which most consumers probably interpret to mean a wage at or above the legal minimum in the coffee-producing country.

Fair Trade relies too much on cooperatives

Fair Trade is criticised for its insistence on coffee and cocoa producers joining a cooperative (producer organisation) in order to be allowed to supply the Fair Trade market. It is felt that this discriminates against those satisfying other standards but who do not want to join a cooperative. It also means leaving out the vast majority of farm workers who work in corporate business organisations. Furthermore, the poorest farmers are the least likely to

---

11   http://www.fairtrade.net/faqs.html?&no_cache=1.

benefit from Fair Trade because they are generally not organised in cooperatives for various reasons – several studies show that partnerships are not formed with the poorest (Hopkins, 2000; Taylor, 2002; Belgian Science Policy, 2005).

Another reason for opposition to cooperatives is because there are often no clear lines of authority or accountability, which makes it difficult for Fair Trade certifiers to police them adequately. It is possible for a cooperative to receive a higher price for its produce and then pay a lower price to the members. It can also buy coffee from the world market at lower prices and sell it as Fair Trade coffee. According to Weber (2007), Fair Trade ensures a minimum price to cooperatives of producers, but not to individual producers. The cooperative serves as an intermediary between the producer and the market. Producers receive the price stipulated in the cooperative's export contract, which must meet or exceed the Fair Trade minimum price, minus the expenses of the cooperative. If the activities of the cooperative are not managed effectively and efficiently then its expenses can be quite high, consuming much of the higher Fair Trade price before it reaches producers. According to Booth (2008: 32), 'co-operatives are a notoriously inefficient form of business organisation, particularly when made up of small producers'. A corruptly managed cooperative can therefore mask the real price of Fair Trade products from individual producers (Howley, 2006).

Weitzman (2006) finds cooperatives lacking in supervising their members. For example, in the case of coffee sold by cooperatives, wage standards apply only to employees of the cooperatives and not to the suppliers. Specific standards regarding temporary workers hired by coffee producers who are members of the cooperative and supply Fair Trade coffee to the cooperative do not exist. The FLO (2006) report merely states: 'where workers are casually hired by farmers themselves, the organisations [cooperatives] should take steps to improve working conditions and to ensure that such workers share the benefits of Fair Trade'.

Another criticism of cooperatives is that the social premiums come to them, and are often not redistributed in projects that directly benefit the producers. Murray et al.'s (2003) study of Latin American coffee cooperatives found that, rather than democratically choosing a community project to fund from the five-cent-per-pound social premium, cooperative leaders have at times made the unilateral decision to use the premium to cover operational costs. In Guatemala, an executive at Fedecocagua, the largest Fair Trade cooperative, admitted that after paying for the cooperative's employees and programmes, nothing of the Fair Trade premium remained to be passed on to the individual farmer (Griffiths, 2009). Murray et al. (2006) also report that field studies on the working of cooperatives show the widespread lack of a clear understanding of Fair Trade among cooperative members. Fair Trade remained an abstract concept to many of them, while their knowledge of organic production was quite well developed. Most activities related to Fair Trade certification and marketing activities are carried out at higher levels in the cooperatives and with distant counterparts and not by producers. Kohler (2006) concurs that, if the cooperative is too big, it increases the distance between decision-makers and members.

Fair Trade organisations use cooperatives because they have traditionally been supplied by small-scale producers and so cooperatives can provide an affordable mechanism for Fair Trade participation. Also, cooperatives provide the kind of central management crucial to checking that the Fair Trade standards are actually being met.

It is true that there is evidence of corruption and mismanagement within Fair Trade cooperatives. At the same time there are examples, albeit few, of successfully managed producer cooperatives that have benefited members in many ways, including in the marketing of their products. These few examples, however, must not distract Fair Trade's proponents from recognising that, on balance, the restriction of cooperatives means that Fair Trade is not able to deal with the very poor unaffiliated producers or corporate farm workers; that poor management of the export process by cooperatives could consume much of the higher Fair Trade price before it reaches producers; and that the lack of democratic processes can hamper the ability to help small-scale producers.

Union Coffee provides an interesting statement about the use of certified Fair Trade coffee. The organisation has impeccable ethical standards but comments:

> We buy specialist coffees of the highest qualities, we travel to farms, get our boots dirty and work closely with farmers. We spend time with them, stay in their houses and are engaged in continuous communication about how we can benefit together.
>
> Over the years, our experience has demonstrated that we have made progress under our own hard work, accomplishing greater improvements in labour standards than by just buying Fairtrade certified coffee. In my opinion Fairtrade was not developed for a business model like ours.

The certified Fair Trade model is undoubtedly limited in its application. This might not be problematic were it not for Fair Trade's efforts to exclude non-certified products in Fair Trade schools, parishes and so on.

Conclusion

Fair Trade is an alternative speciality market and trading channel that offers opportunities for some producers and workers to benefit. It also faces vexing issues, however, such as a disconnect between promotional materials and reality, the difficulty of really engaging economically disadvantaged producers and the costs of organising the Fair Trade system. Any serious advocate of Fair Trade should accept that there are many trading relationships in the free market system that can potentially benefit producers and workers; that free trade is not inherently inequitable; and that the benefits claimed by Fair Trade may also be available in other and at times less costly ways as well.

But the question remains: do the benefits claimed by Fair Trade's proponents really accrue to the producers? Perhaps the most revealing study of the benefits of Fair Trade is that commissioned by the Fairtrade Foundation itself (Nelson and Pound, 2009). It is revealing both for what it finds and because it helps highlight the limitations of all published empirical studies of Fair Trade. Nelson and Pound examine 33 case studies undertaken by other academics – 26 of which were from Latin America and the Caribbean and just seven from Africa. Many of the case studies found some benefit in terms of an improvement in conditions for particular Fair Trade producers. In some cases, there are higher incomes, in others better credit availability, and so on. The hypothetical benefits we have discussed here do seem to be available in practice. There are also signs of 'knock-on' effects from increased buyer competition that benefit non-Fair Trade local producers. It is striking, however, that no research – including this research – has been able to demonstrate the following:

- That the benefits are in any way equivalent to the higher price paid by Northern purchasers so that Fair Trade is an efficient way for the better-off to help poorer producers.
- That the benefits are substantial and greater than the general improvement in living standards that has taken place in recent years in underdeveloped countries – especially in Central America.
- That there is no harm to poor non-Fair Trade producers that are not in the immediate locality of the Fair Trade producers – in particular, that there is no harm to those who take a decision not to participate in Fair Trade on grounds of cost and lack of organisational capacity, who may lose business from the expansion of Fair Trade.
- That the benefits identified in specific case studies can be generalised.
- That the benefits of Fair Trade cannot be realised in other ways.

These things may be impossible to prove but, meanwhile, some humility would be appropriate on the part of Fair Trade proponents. Essentially, the benefits of Fair Trade can only be taken on trust. Consumers may wish to purchase Fair Trade products because they provide certain guarantees about the treatment of primary producers which those consumers subjectively value. It cannot be assumed, however, that those producers are better off as a result of Fair Trade. It should also be understood that the marketing undertaken by Fair Trade organisations is not dispassionate and that the benefits are likely to be 'oversold' without reference to the corresponding costs. This is, of course, the nature of any business organisation and, in that respect, Fair

Trade organisations are no different.

The potential problems of Fair Trade may be oversold too. Some of the problems are theoretical and may apply only if Fair Trade grows substantially. There are certainly important challenges to the Fair Trade movement, however, which cannot be dismissed:

- Fair Trade does not tend to assist the poorest producers, the demand for whose product may actually fall because of Fair Trade.
- The Fair Trade requirements may well reflect the subjective views of Western consumers and not the real needs of poor producers.
- It is not clear that the benefits Fair Trade claims are necessarily achieved in practice.
- Fair Trade can be restrictive in terms of the business models it endorses.
- Fair Trade may impose costs on producers who are simply trying to satisfy the whims of Western consumers.

4 ALTERNATIVES TO FAIR TRADE

Introduction

Fair Trade is not the only initiative that labels products that claim to ensure particular 'social' standards – a number of charitable and non-profit organisations pursue what they describe as a socially conscious business agenda. Indeed, some companies that are profit-making but not profit-maximising may do so too. These initiatives normally define certain social, environmental or quality attributes and have monitoring mechanisms that economic agents along the product supply chain need to fulfil. The scope of these requirements varies greatly across different initiatives, with some providing more flexibility than others. The initiatives usually use some type of labelling, coding and certification to communicate visibly their social agendas to the general public and to increase public confidence in their activities. Governments and international organisations are also engaged in promoting social standards, mainly in the areas of labour and environmental standards. The 2007 G8 summit in Heiligendamm agreed 'on the active promotion of social standards, of corporate social responsibility, and on the need to strengthen social security systems in emerging economies and developing countries'.

In response to a growing demand from consumers an increasing number of business enterprises across the world now pay attention to social and environmental conditions as part of their regular business activities: not always through specially labelled products. This attention of business enterprises is sometimes classified under the general rubric of 'Corporate Social Responsibility' – though this is not necessarily a helpful description. In recent years there has also been a rise in alternative models of ethical trading by companies. Loosely defined, ethical trading means the trading of a product where there is a particular concern in the supply chain over a particular ethical issue (or social standard), such as human rights, the environment, labour conditions and animal wellbeing, and where that product is chosen freely by an individual consumer. The interest in social standards is continuing, though at the same time questions are also being raised about costs, implementation and the real impact of ethical trading on suppliers. Some initiatives for promoting social standards have been more effective than others in achieving their goals.

This chapter discusses the emergence of a range of alternative initiatives for promoting social standards, their implications for producers, traders and consumers, and for the Fair Trade movement. All through this chapter it should be borne in mind that we are not arguing that this or that ethical standard is necessarily a good thing (or even that it is genuinely ethical) – rather we are examining the way in which the market in standards has developed to respond to genuine consumer demand.

Private social labelling initiatives

The 'Rainforest Alliance' and 'Bird Friendly' are initiatives with a main focus on compliance with environmental standards. With regard to coffee, for example, they take into account the degree of shade in coffee plantations. The Bird Friendly label is the most rigorous environmental certification scheme in the coffee sector, since it combines organic standards with shade cover and species richness. The Rainforest Alliance is a comparatively looser certification scheme for coffee, cocoa, ferns, lumber, cut flowers, fruits and tea, which integrates environmental and social concerns. Its standards are often restricted to compliance with local laws, the adoption of good practices for management of agrochemicals and wastes, and keeping a minimum cover of trees. It should not be thought that compliance with local laws is a trivial matter – much forest that is destroyed is done so in contravention of local laws. Whereas the Bird Friendly certification targets numerous North American birdwatchers and bird lovers as supporters, the Rainforest Alliance aims to enlarge the impact of its scheme by encouraging its adoption among large producers, processors and a wide range of end users. It has a history of persuading large-scale corporations to adopt the Rainforest Alliance label as a guarantee of pursuing better business practices to the benefit of their workers, producers and the environment. The market share of the initiatives is still very small though rapidly growing as transnational corporations (TNCs) such as Lavazza, Kraft, Procter & Gamble and Chiquita Brands International have recently started to buy Rainforest Alliance certified coffee and bananas for some of their product lines. The price premium to producers under both the initiatives depends on the market context, but they claim that they have assisted producers to develop better farming practices, to grow better-quality produce, and to establish relationships with buyers, thus enabling their produce to fetch higher prices.

A brand of African coffee, 'Good African Coffee', which has been selling in the supermarkets since 2004, offers a variation of 'Fair Trade' to tap the lucrative niche market for ethically produced goods.[1] The message it wishes to convey is that trade and not aid is the only strategy for African economic and social development, so it approaches the consumer for help through trade and not through charity in terms of paying a premium or making a donation. Good African Coffee attempts to satisfy consumers' demand for ethical trading by: producing and selling the finest African coffees bought directly from the producers; training producers in conservation issues; encouraging organic farming methods; enabling producers to improve on their crop quality and farm productivity; and sharing its profits on an equal basis (that is, 50–50) with producers and their communities for local education and healthcare.

Utz Kapeh is a foundation based in Guatemala and the Netherlands that was set up in 1999 by Ahold, one of the world's largest retail chains, and which later on became an independent initiative. Utz Kapeh means 'good coffee' in the Mayan language. The Utz-code for 'Certified Responsible Coffee' offers assurance of social, environmental and food safety standards in coffee production, and also provides information to the consumer about exactly where their coffee comes from.[2] It aims at mainstreaming certified responsible coffee through the adoption of the label by large retailers and roasters.[3] By promoting its label, the foundation aims

---

1   The coffee is made by the Good African Coffee Company created in 2003 in Uganda by a young entrepreneur, Andrew Rugasira.

2   Utz Kapeh is also developing codes for cocoa, tea and palm oil (http://www. utzcertified.org, accessed 16 December 2008).

3   Douwe Egberts and Ahold, accounting for about 75 per cent of the Dutch market, have adopted the scheme for some of their product lines.

to gain market access at the producer level and as a marketing tool for retailers and roasters. Concerning the pricing scheme, the Utz-foundation charges a very small administration fee to its members without interfering with market pricing. The price premium to coffee producers depends on the market context, but the foundation claims that its assistance has helped producers obtain higher income and prices by improving their productivity and ability to better exploit and access the market.

Starbucks developed socially responsible coffee buying guidelines called Coffee and Farmer Equity (CAFÉ) Practices as part of its 'Preferred Supplier Program' in 2001.[4] Starbucks sources sustainably grown and processed coffee by evaluating the economic, social and environmental aspects of coffee production against a set of criteria defined by the CAFÉ Practices. The Practices define sustainability as an economically viable model that addresses the social and environmental needs of all the participants in the supply chain from producer to consumer. Monitoring of Starbucks' criteria is carried out by third parties and the costs are covered by producers. Producers participating in the programme, however, normally earn price premiums. Starbucks offers producers a premium over the market price based on a points system for environmental (50 per cent), social (30 per cent) and economic (20 per cent) criteria. The premium, though discretionary on the part of Starbucks, is well known for being quite handsome (Tallontire and Vorley, 2005).

The Common Code for the Coffee Community (4C), launched in 2003, aims at becoming an industry-wide applied code.[5] Its

---

4   The CAFÉ Practices were developed in collaboration with Scientific Certification Systems (SCS), a third-party evaluation and certification firm.

5   www.sustainable-coffee.net.

FAIR TRADE WITHOUT THE FROTH

basic element is the voluntary code of conduct covering 30 social, environmental and economic practices. The code used in the coffee sector guides all actors in the coffee supply chain – farmers, plantations, producer organisations, estates, mills, exporters and traders – on the way towards what it describes as more sustainable production, post-harvest processing and trading of coffee. Once the participants have eliminated ten practices they define as 'Unacceptable' in the code, they have to continually improve their practices in order to comply with the rest of the code. Actors who don't exclude 'Unacceptable' practices cannot be members of the 4C. An independent third-party verification agency checks compliance with the code, emphasising the responsibility of all actors along the chain.

The code promotes what it regards as environmental sustainability through reducing the use of hazardous agrochemicals and protecting tropical rainforests. It also organises support services for producers through networks that provide access to training programmes, promotes good agricultural and management practices, facilitates information exchange and strengthens the self-organisation of farmers. It expects to improve producers' income and living conditions through cost reductions, quality improvements, optimisation of the supply chain, improved marketing conditions and better access to markets and trade credit facilities. The trade and industry members of 4C commit themselves to buying increasing amounts of 4C coffee over time and cover with their membership fees the costs of third-party verification and the 4C support services. The 4C system does not use a logo or seal on coffee packs. What is unique about 4C is its flexible design and moderate entry level, which make it easily accessible for all actors, at the same time making sure that they embark on the road towards sustainability and commit themselves to continual improvement. Further, the 4C approach is non-competitive and can be used in conjunction with any other existing social standards.

The Sustainable Agriculture Initiative (SAI), created by major transnational food corporations in 2002, is a platform for the development of sustainable agricultural practices that are harmonised along the food chain (as well as in compliance with trade policies and regulations) through activities centred on knowledge-building, awareness-raising, stakeholder involvement and technical support. The promotion of sustainable agriculture as both a long term-goal and a continual learning process is expected to enable local communities to better maintain their livelihood, safeguard their environment and improve their well-being. For example, the Coffee Platform aims at improving the quality of coffee, reducing oversupply of coffee and protecting the environment, thus improving the livelihoods of sustainable coffee producers. The initiative draws on financial support from big firms and the international community: Ecom, Efico, Kraft, Nestlé, Neumann Kaffee Gruppe, Sara Lee, Tchibo and Volcafe are active members of the Coffee Platform. The participation of producers in the Platform is voluntary. Like the 4C, SAI can be used in conjunction with any other internal codes or any other standards.

In response to the proliferation of private social labelling or certification initiatives there have been some attempts at their merger, but without much success. When the national initiatives of Fair Trade created the FLO in 1997 it was thought that some of the existing socially concerned labels would merge with them. Again, when the 4C was launched in 2003, there was some discussion about the social labels promoting 'good practices' converging within a 4C common code. So far this has not happened because most social labels claim that their objectives, operating mechanisms and target audiences are different. The proliferation of labels continues: there is talk about a low-air-miles label, a goods-produced-without-child-labour label and so on.

The rise of corporate social standards

COM (2001) defines 'Corporate Social Responsibility' or CSR as 'a concept whereby companies integrate social and environmental concerns in their business operations on a voluntary basis'. It suggests that companies are responsible for their actions in a sphere wider than that covered by the mere profit-and-loss statement. Many major corporations around the world now seek to address issues of 'social responsibility'. Given extensive concern over quality (including health) and safety issues as well as respecting the International Labour Organization Core Labour Standards, most companies have in place policies addressing these concerns. It is not the purpose of this monograph to go into the rights and wrongs of this agenda, and it certainly does not propose legislation in this field. The widespread development of CSR over the last decade or so, however, is relevant to the Fair Trade and ethical labelling movement.

In the UK the Ethical Trading Initiative's (ETI) Base Code was developed by a consortium of companies and trade unions anxious to improve working conditions and human rights in the workplace. The ETI Base Code focus is chiefly on organised labour and workplace practices, but many companies go beyond this and have instituted policies addressing other trading and environmental conditions (Tallontire and Vorley, 2005). Many companies subscribe to the Social Accountability 8000 (SA8000) standard, which has been developed as a voluntary universal standard for companies interested in auditing and certifying labour practices in their facilities and those of their suppliers and vendors through an independent third party.

More than half of the world's biggest companies reveal details of their environmental and social performance (Buck, 2005). Accounting firm KPMG found in its study that 52 per cent of the 250 largest corporations published CSR reports and that they covered a much wider range of issues in 2005 than they had covered in 2002 (Grodnik and Conroy, 2007). Independent agencies such as Calvert Financial Services now issue regular assessments of the social, environmental and governance performance of many companies. These assessments include the full range of activities from workplace and business practices, human rights behaviour and environmental responsibility to community relations (CSRwire, 2006).

The CSR policies of many companies also take the form of promoting alternative models of ethical trading. This is reflected in the proliferation of certification and product seals adopted by corporate entities (Busch and Bain, 2004; Hughes, 2005). Firms follow a range of mechanisms for imposing and auditing ethical trading standards. These efforts could be through self-regulation or first-party certifications, where firms use internal mechanisms for standard-setting and monitoring. They rely on their own brand reputations in assuring consumers of the validity of their CSR claims. To bolster the legitimacy of their claims, many corporations pursue stakeholder standard-setting and third-party certifications that shift responsibility for standard-setting and monitoring to stakeholders and outside agencies respectively.

A question frequently asked is why do companies engage in CSR? The reasons for this can be many. The highly visible brand names of large corporations create key pressure points for them. Most of them thrive on promoting their brand names, so building the brand is their main effort, and they seek to protect it. To the degree that the symbolic and financial value of global brands has risen over recent years, so too has corporate vulnerability to image damage (Lury, 2004). The Internet has created new mechanisms for virtually instant global awareness of charges of irresponsibility such as environmental and human rights violations (Conroy, 2001; Grodnik and Conroy, 2007). Seizing this opportunity, NGOs and social movement groups at times pursue a powerful strategy of 'naming and shaming' – publicising corporate practices for not conforming with their social and environmental visions. Undoubtedly, this puts pressure on companies.

It would be wrong, however, to assign this as the main reason for companies embracing CSR. More important is the fact that companies operate within the market, and hence it is good business practice for them to respond to the social and environmental preferences and concerns of consumers and civil society. It would seem that expectations with regard to corporate behaviour have increased, and it is in the interests of companies to respond. The fact that some consumers are willing to see beyond the quality and price of products and exercise preferences about other issues when buying products is perfectly reasonable, and the signals that companies receive cannot be ignored (Castaldo et al., 2009).

Some companies may embrace CSR policies to facilitate price discrimination. This arises because some consumers are ready to pay a higher price for products coming from companies they see as socially responsible, and these consumers may well have a relatively price-inelastic demand (Creyer and Ross, 1997; Ellen et al., 2000; Mohr et al., 2001). Finally, as noted by Donaldson and Preston (1995: 67), some companies may embrace CSR even if it is not in the interests of their shareholders to do so. The basis of social responsibility for such companies is the recognition that 'the interests of all stakeholders are of intrinsic value, that is, each group of stakeholders merits consideration for its own sake and not merely because of its ability to further the interest of some other group, such as the shareowners'. This does, though, raise questions about corporate governance and the accountability of management to shareholders.

While studies of the effect of CSR on consumer purchasing preferences have been inconclusive, it is clear that a positive CSR reputation can be used to build brand loyalty and to market products that embody ethical and social values. These products will primarily appeal to consumers who are particularly sensitive to these values, and CSR can be a source of competitive advantage for companies marketing these products (Porter and Kramer, 2006; Castaldo et al., 2009). Whatever the motivation for companies engaging in CSR, the fact is that CSR is now integral to many businesses and it is therefore wrong to assume that the ethical, environmental and health values are associated only with social movement groups. CSR has made it possible for these values to be transformed into key facets of corporate profitability, branding and marketing (Raynolds and Wilkinson, 2007).

Government-regulated social standards

Organic certification is an initiative for promoting sustainable environmental practices. It usually requires meeting rigorous standards for recycling wastes, reducing water pollution, chemical inputs and erosion and improving soil quality. Unlike other private labelling initiatives, organic certification is subject to a governmental process of regulation in many countries. In Europe organic food production and marketing have been strictly regulated since 1993, when EC Council Regulation 2092/91 became effective. The regulation and its subsequent amendments set out the inputs and practices which may be used in organic farming and the inspection system which must be put in place. This regulation also applies to processing, processing aids and ingredients in organic foods. All foods sold as organic must originate from growers, processors and importers who are registered with a government-approved certification body and subject to regular inspection.

There is little international harmonisation of organic standards, and this has led to a proliferation of organic certifying organisations. This means that if producers are to gain access to different foreign markets they may be required to adopt different organic certification seals. The adoption of organic certification does involve costs, but it offers a premium to the farmer, depending on market interactions between buyers and suppliers.

When it comes to standards in the areas of the treatment of labour and the environment (such as in the context of climate change) government-established compulsory legal minimum standards are also in place. The International Labour Organisation (ILO) Core Labour Standards have to be respected by all nation members.[6] They include freedom of association and the effective recognition of the right to collective bargaining; the

---

6   The ILO had 183 nation members as of December 2009.

elimination of all forms of forced or compulsory labour; the effective abolition of child labour; and the elimination of discrimination in respect of employment and occupation. A growing number of multilateral and bilateral agreements also refer to labour standards. The North American Free Trade Agreement (NAFTA), the Southern Common Market (MERCOSUR) and the Central American Free Trade Agreement (CAFTA) make references to the international labour standards.

The US and EU bilateral trade and investment agreements already imply treatment-of-labour clauses. From 2009 the EU linked its new Generalised System of Preferences (GSP plus) tariff preferences and development assistance to the implementation of the eight ILO fundamental conventions.[7] Many international organisations, such as the Asian Development Bank (ADB) and the International Finance Corporation (IFC), have adopted the ILO fundamental conventions in their agreements. There are also multilateral protocols that exist in the area of the environment. These require commitments from participating nations to enforce environmental controls to achieve agreed pollution reduction targets. There is pressure from the international community on countries to conform to these protocols.

There has been an emergence of initiatives with different levels of commitments from governments for promoting certain social standards among business enterprises. The OECD Guidelines for Multinational Enterprises (Revision 2000) provide voluntary principles and standards for responsible business conduct in all the major areas of business ethics, including employment and industrial relations, human rights, environment, information

---

7   The GSP is the system of preferential trading arrangements through which countries extend preferential access to their markets to developing countries.

disclosure, combating bribery, consumer interests, science and technology, competition, and taxation. The guidelines do not apply only to companies' operations in their countries of origin but to their activities worldwide. They also encourage companies' subcontractors explicitly to implement them. The guidelines, though not legally binding on companies, are legally binding on governments. Governments of adhering countries commit to promoting them among multinational enterprises operating in or from their territories. More and more countries have adopted them – they include all OECD countries and eleven non-OECD countries: Argentina, Brazil, Chile, Estonia, Egypt, Israel, Latvia, Lithuania, Peru, Romania and Slovenia (OECD, 2000).

Clearly, government-mandated standards might be an alternative to private labelling initiatives: indeed, government standards might crowd out private initiative. Steinrucken and Jaenichen (2007) do not favour widespread use of legal minimum standards as an alternative to voluntary standards for a variety of reasons. They argue that it is likely to lead to trade protectionism (for example, through lobbying by interest groups for standards to be imposed on products produced in another country). Also, if the government imposes standards then the costs of enforcement are borne by taxpayers and not by producers and consumers of relevant products. In the case of standards based on voluntary initiative, only those buyers who are willing to pay for the standards are charged with the additional expenses, and different standards can develop to meet different consumer needs.

There may also be a tendency for government standards to become mandatory (especially given the influence of protectionist lobbies) whereas, with voluntary initiatives, consumers still have the opportunity to buy products in the traditional market.

Steinrucken and Jaenichen's (ibid.) points are valid, but there are questions to be raised about voluntary standards and their implementation.

The proliferation of standards and labels raises many questions

The rise of voluntary social standards – or the privatisation of regulation and labelling – for a wide range of products, as a complement to government laws and regulations, is seen by some as an unnecessary evolution of the statutory regulatory framework. Private sector bodies such as the EurepGAP, the International Social and Environmental Accreditation and Labelling (ISEAL) Alliance and the FLO are engaged in developing best-practice codes for the design and implementation of social and environmental standards for the certification of agricultural and other products around the globe. They are advocates for voluntary standards as an effective mechanism for achieving positive social and environmental change – though these bodies do also campaign for statutory regulation.

Businesses and countries may regard private social standards and labels as an imposition by industrialised countries. There can be much tension involved in the development of standards and the indicators used to measure them: who are standards for? How and by whom are they created? How are they maintained? The strategies, codes and auditing methods of private standards setters impose costs on producers in the developing world. They may be regarded as reflecting the vision of Northern consumers and NGOs, and doubts are raised about their ability to involve Southern producers and consumers in the shaping of the standards. Consequently standards such as Fair Trade can be seen as a subtle form of protectionism. There is a fear that campaigning from social movement groups could result in the linkage of social standards to trade agreements, thus forming yet another non-tariff barrier to entry into the European market, along with the existing technical and health barriers to trade (African Fair Trade Symposium Statement, 2006). Private labelling initiatives are also blamed for preventing developing countries from developing their own social standards and practices that are more relevant to their circumstances. Hughes (2004) identifies this as one of the main challenges facing voluntary labelling and regulatory schemes.

Private standards have also been criticised for altering traditional governance practices in rural communities by imposing paper burdens and externally designed procedures and practices (Mutersbaugh, 2002). For instance, if the standards include conditions that imply higher costs for employing labour, then this could result in a shift in the factor input combination in favour of a more capital-intensive production method.

Labels are supposed to be a way to discipline the flows of distorted information and manipulative images that are used in promotion campaigns and advertisements: they act as summary information that is certified by an independent source. But when labels themselves proliferate and are used as ad hoc marketing tools they can confuse consumers and undermine consumer confidence in the labels (Lewin et al., 2004). Lately there has been an increase in competition between alternative labels. For example, it is common to find coffee with different social labels – Bird-Friendly, Rainforest Alliance, the Starbucks code, the SAI code, Utz Kapeh, 4C and Fair Trade – on supermarket shelves. Are consumers really able to distinguish the information embodied in these different labels? This can cause a clash between schemes, and they may be blamed for being misleading (Murdian and Pelupessy, 2005). Some environmental or similar labels embody complex or profuse information that lay consumers are usually not able to process (Morris et al., 1995; Aldrich, 1999; Karl and Orwat, 1999). The Bird-Friendly and Rainforest Alliance labels share a common challenge of communicating a relatively complex property of coffee cultivation (shade) and its very relevant environmental implications to the general public. Even governments and civil society are at a loss when it comes to defining how social standards, laws and regulations relate to one another.

It is alleged that some social labels are void of any substantial content but mislead consumers. Kohler (2006) feels that the ambiguity often arises from the use of terms such as 'sustainability' or 'responsibility' or 'fair', which are vague enough to let people believe what marketing experts want them to believe. This is clear when examining the marketing rhetoric and pricing schemes of some of the most widespread labels. A flaw of the Fair Trade concept is that consumers cannot assess whether the 'fair' conditions claimed by it are respected (Gebben and Gitsham, 2007) – or whether they are 'fair' in that they actually help the people they are intended to help without adverse consequences. A related problem is that the bureaucratic monitoring procedures involved in labelling may undermine the values the label seeks to promote.

Furthermore, there is no process of independent regulation of private social labelling initiatives – though standard contract law, consumer protection law and so on apply. There is an information asymmetry between the buyers and the sellers of social labelling products. Buyers need to trust the label and this trust is nourished by the information they have about the initiative, by stories and media reports they read about it, by endorsements from various sources, by campaigning, by the accountability and transparency exhibited by the initiatives, and other considerations such as who retails the products (Castaldo et al., 2009). There is, however, little chance of verifying the claims.

Even systems offering a premium, such as Fair Trade's, do not offer a much better scenario, particularly when it comes to the participation of small-scale farmers. According to Kohler (2006), standards always assist some producers while excluding others who are not in a position to access the benefits. Some would argue that these codes benefit a resourceful elite rather than the producers in general.

Fair Trade compared with other overtly socially responsible business practice

Fair Trade claims to be the only social label that offers a financial counterpart (premium) above the market price in order to help producers. The other social labels do not explicitly ask for a price premium for producers but claim to support them by building their capacity to compete and interact in the market. For example, coffee certified by organic and shade-grown labels (Bird-Friendly, Rainforest Alliance) is sold at a price above the market price; in turn, part of the enhanced price arises because of the higher transformation costs in these kinds of cultures, and part of it is because of the marketing advantages derived from using the label. Therefore, even if other labels do not specifically ask for a price premium, as in the case of Fair Trade, it must be recognised that the derived marketing advantage for producers leads to a more or less similar result – it makes the brand more attractive and leads to a higher price for producers. Furthermore, as we noted earlier, the price premium actually received by Fair Trade producers can be far lower than is commonly perceived. Of course, there are also other ways producers can receive an enhanced price and profit for their produce, such as by moving into speciality brands of coffee that command a higher market price.

Steinrucken and Jaenichen (2007) report that business buyers of coffee and other products may also pay extra for labelled coffee just as end consumers will. The purchasing organisation could then generate extra profitability because the company obtains a positive image and their end consumers may be more willing to use the company. One example of this is the franchise company Starbucks, which pays more for coffee than the world market price. Some supporters of Fair Trade have suggested, however, that Starbucks is paying the higher price to assure future supplies of quality coffee, and that there is no premium involved. This would be conventional business practice. On the one hand, the criticism, if valid, is pertinent because it would mean that Starbucks was not making any additional sacrifice to help producers. On the other hand, though, it is a further demonstration that normal self-interested business practice leads to market outcomes not dissimilar to those that Fair Trade attempts to achieve.

The bottom line is that the use of labelled products and what may seem like the adoption of overtly socially responsible business practices are often simply good business practices for companies. Berndt (2007) finds that, in the case of coffee, companies such as Starbucks, Allegro and Peet's are encouraging business practices that go a long way to improving the lives of small farmers by providing higher income from coffee production as well as long-term and stable business ties between coffee producers and coffee companies. Even if the focus of the companies is promoting an excellent product that the consumer wants in a competitive market, or even if the motive behind the adoption of overtly socially responsible business practice is corporate and brand reputation, it is still good business for both the buyer and the producer. Overtly socially responsible business practice need not be at cross-purposes with long-run profit maximisation: competition, efficiency and social goals can complement each other in the long run. As Jeff Teter, president of Allegro Coffee, explains: 'We have growers we have ongoing relationships with. We spend money back on projects in the growers' community ... We're doing it because we feel it is the right thing. But it's also good business.'

Fair Trade claims to be the only label that specifies a floor price for coffee and which explicitly encourages long-term relationships between buyers and producers to offer stability of income to producers.[8] Although most other social labelling initiatives do not specify a floor price, they do commit themselves to long-term commercial relationship between buyers and producers. For example, the Utz Kapeh and the Starbuck Preferred Supplier Program offer stability to suppliers through longer-term contracts. Moreover, it is not uncommon for conventional market buyers to enter into long-term contracts with sellers (producers) to ensure a stable flow of supplies, as well as a stable flow of income to the seller. Some of them even offer pre-financing to producers, which, in practice, is not different from Fair Trade's facilitation of credit facilities.

---

8   Above we noted that Fair Trade's claim of offering stability of income to producers was an exaggeration and impractical for producers.

For example, some coffee millers in Costa Rica offer producers a pre-announced guaranteed minimum price and credit facilities for buying coffee, and if at the time of purchase the market price is higher, they pay the higher price. They are able to do so by offsetting their assumed price risk in the New York Board of Trade coffee futures market (Mohan, 2007a). This has helped them to develop long-term relationships with producers for an assured supply of coffee to the mutual benefit of the millers and producers. Similarly, it is not uncommon for grain traders to offer credit and/or minimum prices with assurance of purchase to farmers. Again, they are able to do so by hedging their assumed price risk through forward and futures contracts in the commodity derivative markets for these products. We should recognise that conventional business relationships also offer mechanisms that can provide stability of income to producers.

Some proponents of Fair Trade are concerned about some companies adopting a social label for only one or a few of their product lines in order to leverage their social reputation (Ransom, 2005). This leads to a situation where consumers may believe that a company is generally following certain practices that are overtly socially responsible because of a reputation that is gained from practice across a small proportion of the product range.[9] It can be argued, however, that the companies involved are simply trying to promote variety in their product lines. The use of social labels involves additional costs of inspection, certification and organisation of the supply chain. This may be attractive only to consumers of a few high-value niche brands.

Fair Trade and other social initiatives differ in regard to the

9   Nestlé's Partner's Blend Fair Trade label coffee or Kenco's Rainforest Alliance certified brand are examples of the product lines that are under social labelling.

stringency of standards. The Starbucks code, Rainforest Alliance, the SAI code, Utz Kapeh and the 4C have very similar types of social, environmental and economic performance 'minimum standards'. The standards are meant to exclude the worst practices and are generally set at a level so as to achieve minimum levels of good practice. This means that entry barriers are low and strong coordination and monitoring systems for ensuring compliance of the standards are not required. On the other hand, Fair Trade and organic labels and to some extent the Bird Friendly label set more rigorous standards and target niche market segments. This requires a higher degree of exchange of information, regulation and monitoring, as well as stronger coordination between producers and buyers to ensure compliance. In turn, this can mean that the reach of these schemes could be constrained in terms of the total number of producers (and the total volume of the product) who can feasibly be involved. Fair Trade is the only social labelling scheme that for some products, such as coffee and cocoa, requires that a producer cooperative acts as medium between producer and buyer. Other labelling schemes are open to producers, cooperatives and large estates.

Fairtrade[10] 'absolutism'

We have seen that there are a variety of standard market mechanisms as well as new breeds of labelled products that are trying to provide for consumers and producers particular characteristics within the production process which are mutually beneficial.

---

10   Here 'Fairtrade' rather than 'Fair Trade' is generally used because the critique specifically refers to officially labelled products of the Fairtrade Foundation or similar bodies in other countries.

Despite this, Fairtrade rhetoric is often seen as an unreasonable smear campaign against high-end marketers and retailers who resist the Fairtrade model and seems to implicitly deny the existence of other labelled products. Global Exchange, an international human rights organisation and Fairtrade retailer, adopted this stance by declaring that almost all coffee that is not Fairtrade exploits producers and workers. Sometimes deeply partial statements are made by advocates of Fairtrade: Booth (2008) says, 'for example, in my own diocese – the Catholic diocese of Arundel and Brighton – I have been told that not to buy Fair Trade products is a sin worse than theft; that not buying Fair Trade products is making a deliberate choice to take from the poor; and that one should never buy products that appear to have the virtues of Fair Trade but do not have the official Fairtrade mark: this is actually stated on the diocesan website'.

The Whole Planet Foundation president Philip Sansone explains that Fairtrade farmers might receive some initial benefits from the programme, but other factors must also be considered when looking at the big picture of eliminating poverty. When Fairtrade advocates communicate the message to customers that products that are not labelled Fairtrade are based on the exploitation of peasants by an unjust and exploitative economic system, that is simply untrue, deceptive and unfair to the vast majority of producers who market their products in the conventional market. The Foundation president finds no merit in buying Fair Trade products over an equally attractive competitive product, which probably costs less because it doesn't support the 'Fair Trade tax'.

In 2000, activist groups including Global Exchange launched an attack on Starbucks for exploiting farmers. Yet, given its size, Starbucks is likely to have done far more than Fairtrade to improve the lot of coffee growers in the countries from which it purchases coffee. Starbucks buys 2.2 per cent of the world's coffee production and it fuels demand for high-priced speciality coffee.[11] By focusing on quality, coffee outlets such as Starbucks, Costa, Allegro and Peet's are encouraging business practices through entrepreneurship that can lead to much higher margins for farmers. This goes a long way to improving the lives of small farmers by providing long-term stable business ties between coffee producers and coffee distributors. Speciality and high-quality coffee have always fetched above-average prices, and the speciality revolution has probably increased prices far more than any other movement (Howley, 2006).[12] *The Economist* (2007) observed that investments in high-quality coffees in Brazil can increase a farmer's profits by 50 per cent.

Boudreaux (2007) documents how the high-quality and speciality coffee industry in Rwanda is helping to change lives because companies reward producers for supplying quality coffee through offering them prices above the market price for standard brands, together with longer-term contracts. Many buyers extend their activities to training producers to grow coffee that fetches a higher premium. It is common for them to send coffee experts to teach producers how to increase the quality of their crop. By growing such coffee, producers are earning more. In 2005, ordinary-grade Rwandan coffee sold for approximately US$1.30 per kilo; fully

11   Ironically, Starbucks now markets Fair Trade coffee as one of its lines and is the largest purchaser of Fair Trade coffee in North America, although Fair Trade coffee comprises only 3.7 per cent of the company's purchases (Berndt, 2007). This percentage may have increased since the date of this study.

12   Jeff Teter from Allegro Coffee puts it: 'To get great quality coffee, you pay a lot more than what the Fair Trade floor prices are. One hundred percent of what we bought was more than $1.41 ... It's not the Fair Trade price; it's much higher.'

washed higher-quality coffee, on the other hand, was selling for more than $2.50 per kilo. In a truly remarkable achievement, in September 2007 importers paid as much as $55.00 per kilo for the best Rwandan coffee. A 2006 report to USAID notes that 'approximately 50,000 households have seen their incomes from coffee production double, and some 2,000 jobs have been created at coffee washing stations' (ibid.: 14).

It is therefore both simplistic and populist to assert that the production and purchase of Fairtrade products somehow lies on a higher moral plane than other business activity or that it corrects inequitable trade. Berndt (2007) observes that such a claim is problematic also because Fairtrade is neither specific about what constitutes greater equity nor is the idea incorporated into its rules in a concrete and measurable manner. Moreover, promoting an overt social agenda is not unique to Fairtrade: as has been noted, several social movements and corporate entities also have an overt social agenda. While Fairtrade producers benefit from the alternative trade channel and the relationship with buyers, so do those involved with many other labelling movements or those who produce for niche markets. Furthermore, producers and workers in developing countries also benefit from conventional trading, and it is inappropriate on the part of Fairtrade enthusiasts to undermine this benefit for promoting Fairtrade.

Indeed, it would be legitimate to express concern about the 'market power' of the various Fairtrade organisations. The Fairtrade Foundation has persuaded many towns, schools, universities and parishes to become 'Fair Trade'. There are a number of requirements that have to be passed. For example, schools have to do the following:

- commit to selling, promoting and using Fairtrade products as much as possible;
- ensure that students learn about Fairtrade in at least three subjects in each of two year groups;[13]
- take action for Fairtrade at least once a term in the school and once a year in the wider community.

Whether a school should be taking action to partially educate its pupils in such subtle and subjective areas of economics is a matter which we will not pursue. The requirement to commit to selling and promoting Fairtrade products (that is those labelled by FLO), however, is a requirement across schools, parishes and so on. Fairtrade is actively seeking a monopoly on those products it certifies to the exclusion not just of non-certified or non-labelled products but also of other labelling movements that claim a special ethical status, such as the Rainforest Alliance. If Rainforest Alliance products, for example, are not to find it more difficult to find a place in Fairtrade schools, towns and parishes, producers will have to sign up to multiple labelling schemes at considerable explicit and implicit expense.

Conclusion

In recent years there has been an emergence of a large number of initiatives to promote overtly 'socially responsible' production and for the trading of products. In particular the food sector has witnessed a proliferation of private social labelling initiatives that extend beyond organic production and Fair Trade, though

---

13 Unsurprisingly, this is from materials provided by the Foundation or its supporting bodies.

arguably these two are still the most well known. Also there has been a rise of approaches to overtly ethical trading and the development of CSR practices within large corporations. To the extent that these initiatives promote particular social and environmental practices that are attractive to consumers and beneficial to producers they should be welcomed. They are not, however, without their costs, and they face limitations and challenges. It should also be kept in mind that government regulations also exist to promote social standards, particularly in the areas of labour and environment.

Fair Trade is a private social labelling initiative of this type that promotes a particular social agenda while providing certain types of financial infrastructure for producers. Arguably, it is preferable to state-sponsored standards that can lead lobby groups to pressurise governments to use them for protectionist purposes to the serious detriment of poor producer countries. It is certainly simplistic to assert that Fair Trade somehow lies on a higher moral plane as compared with other social initiatives, or that it necessarily lies on a higher moral plane than normal business practices. Furthermore, there are no objective and substantial studies that estimate the benefits and costs of different initiatives. Moreover, the emergence of these initiatives should not distract us from the fact that conventional trading too can promote socially responsible practices, including the furthering of the interests of producers and stakeholders through long-term relationships based on mutual respect, and that it can do so without some of the costs and limitations of the private labelling initiatives. We should also be aware that institutions that promote private labelling initiatives have their own self-interest – marketing statements should not necessarily be taken at face value. It is legitimate for consumers to question the claims of the different labelling initiatives (Rainforest Alliance, Bird-Friendly, Fair Trade and so on) – some of these will have specific and more easily verifiable aims attractive to particular consumers; others will have more diffuse aims.

5 FAIR TRADE AS A LONG-TERM DEVELOPMENT STRATEGY FOR THE GLOBAL SOUTH

1. 'Fairtrade is a strategy for poverty alleviation and sustainable development. Its purpose is to create opportunities for producers and workers who have been economically disadvantaged or marginalized by the conventional trading system' (Fairtrade Foundation).[1]

2. 'Seven million disadvantaged producers, workers and their families are benefiting from Fairtrade' (Fairtrade Foundation).[2]

3. 'The fact that Fairtrade has allowed producers to transform their lives also shows that the current system of trade is not working. The price of coffee didn't plummet in recent years simply due to oversupply: oversupply was created when dozens of countries were forced to move into cash crops as a condition for loans from the World Bank. The price of sugar hasn't hit rock bottom simply because of an oversupply: oversupply was created by trade rules allowing huge subsidies to be provided to American sugar producers' (Fairtrade Foundation).[3]

4. 'It is the claim that free trade is the only way to tackle poverty

---

1   http://www.fairtrade.org.uk/SearchResults.aspx?searchterm=strategy+for+po
    verty+alleviation.
2   http://www.fairtrade.org.uk/get_involved/trade_justice.aspx.
3   Ibid.

that renders it nonsense in the real world of extreme global inequality. Those of us who have had the privilege of seeing and hearing at first hand the difference that Fairtrade makes to poor communities are not going to be persuaded otherwise by the rehashing of simplistic economic theories' (Fairtrade Foundation).[4]

Introduction

Fair Trade claims to be a distinctive market-based mechanism with an explicit provision for the redistribution of income to primary product producers in developing countries. This claim has been criticised: questions can be raised about the high cost of the Fair Trade mechanism and its capability to target marginalised producers and workers given its complex requirements; there are concerns that much of the gain from the Fair Trade price premium goes to the Fair Trade bureaucracy rather than to the producer; and there are strong objections that Fair Trade campaigning distorts the benefits for producers and workers from conventional international trade and other market mechanisms.

Notwithstanding the above-mentioned limitations, Fair Trade is now an integral part of the market system and is probably here to stay. It is an alternative speciality market trade channel within the market system that offers more choices to certain producers and workers and possibilities for some of them to avail themselves of extra benefits from relationships with buyers and a captive market of price-inelastic consumers. This, in many respects, is similar to organic or other social labelling initiatives.

---

4   http://www.fairtrade.org.uk/press_office/press_releases_and_statements/ feb_2008/response_to_adam_smith_insititute_report.aspx.

Many Fair Trade proponents, however, believe the movement to be a long-term movement to assist the development of poor countries. Fair Trade is not regarded as a niche market beneficial to some producers or consumers: it is regarded as underpinning the process of development in the underdeveloped world. This objective is stated, for example, on the FLO's website (section entitled 'Our Vision'): 'We believe that trade can be a fundamental driver of poverty reduction and greater sustainable development, but only if it is managed for that purpose, with greater equity and transparency than is currently the norm.'[5] The World Fair Trade Organisation (WFTO) website posts the 'Charter of Fair Trade Principles', which claims, 'Fair Trade is fundamentally a response to the failure of conventional trade to deliver sustainable livelihoods and development opportunities to people in the *poorest* countries in the world'[6] (emphasis added). It seems that the FLO marketing literature has hit home. The TNS CAPI OmniBus survey showed that over 90 per cent of those recognising the label believed that Fair Trade represents an improved development strategy compared with free trade.[7] The quotes from the Fairtrade Foundation at the head of this chapter show the ambitions that the Foundation holds for Fair Trade and the perceived limitations of existing trade policy. This chapter critically discusses whether Fair Trade is a development strategy.

---

5   FLO website, http://www.fairtrade.net/our_vision.html.
6   WFTO website, http://www.wfto.com/index.php?option=com_content&task=blogcategory&id=11&Itemid=12.
7   This survey is highlighted in the Fairtrade Foundation press release 'Awareness of FAIRTRADE Mark leaps to 70%', 10 May 2008.

Does Fair Trade really counteract the so-called social problems caused or revealed by international trade?

The growth of international trade and globalisation is widely accepted as being instrumental in promoting development and prosperity across the world, but it also attracts criticism from anti-globalisation protesters for causing certain social problems. At times Fair Trade campaigners and supporters offer Fair Trade as a solution to some of these problems. An argument put forward against international trade is the lack of transparency in international commodity chains. It is posited that the consumer is making consumption choices based on imperfect information, and that commodities sold in the marketplace are made to appear independent of the people and the environments that produced them. This invisibility of the components of the production chain permits, it is argued, the persistence of socially unjust practices, such as the use of slave and child labour in the harvesting of cacao, documented in West Africa and in the Ivory Coast in particular (Tiffen, 2002).

Fair Trade labelling could potentially provide some additional information about the product or the production process. This reduces monitoring costs for buyers and also enables some suppliers of products to demonstrate their skills and standards of production. There are also other ways of preventing such practices. For instance, governments and civil society play an important role; the packaging and labelling of products also provide information to buyers depending on the legal disclosure requirements in the country in question. A positive trend is that with globalisation (Internet, travel, media) instances of such practices attract prompt international exposure and pressure. Companies are increasingly sensitive to such pressure. Nevertheless, Fair

Trade is one channel by which greater consumer information can be communicated, though we should beware of Fair Trade absolutism.

Another criticism of the way international trading relations are structured is that significant elements of value-added sequencing, in which substantial profits may accrue, tend to occur outside the immediate production area. As a result the producer of primary products cannot capture the added value that is captured by others farther up the product development chain (Farnworth and Goodman, 2006). For example, current estimates suggest that coffee-producing countries capture a mere 10 per cent of the value of the global coffee market, which is worth upwards of $80 billion a year (Oxfam, 2002). Specifically, as a recent documentary about the coffee industry in Ethiopia shows (Black Gold, 2006), of the £14 paid for a pound of speciality coffee at the supermarket, 59 pence is the maximum that would go to the Ethiopian farmers for the raw coffee beans (Castle, 2006). Again, the Fair Trade model does little to alter this, though it does something.

The solution to this problem is structural transformation. This should include the removal of trade barriers but also the creation of better conditions for general economic development within poorer countries so that they can migrate up the value chain and so that labour, in general, becomes more productive. In fact, there is a positive trend of growing vertical integration in commodity markets because of market liberalisation and globalisation (Krivonos, 2004; Mohan and Russell, 2008). This has improved producers' access to international markets and has also encouraged, depending on the comparative advantage, greater value addition nearer the production area. Berndt's (2007) study of Guatemalan and Costa Rican coffee farmers finds that some small farmers have invested in their own 'micro-mills' so they can capture the profits of this second step in the coffee supply chain.

It is also argued that 'upstream' actors in buyer-driven chains – the end users and the supermarkets – exert economic and quality control over the entire chain to the detriment of downstream stakeholders. For example, owing to their power, end users and supermarkets are able to pass the costs of demand instability on to producers. In so doing, they shift economic risk down the commodity chain to small-scale farmers and workers. Labour costs are driven down and many of the non-wage costs of employment are avoided (Barrientos and Dolan, 2006). Here again, Fair Trade can do little to help where these problems are caused by the structural nature of the economies concerned. If labour productivity were generally higher in poor countries then labour would migrate out of the production of primary products and into other economic activity. This would raise the price that buyers would have to pay for the labour element of primary products.

Yet another criticism of international trade is that it brings about increased competition and that this worsens the economic conditions of the weakest participants in international trade, particularly the marginal producers in the Third World (Steinrucken and Jaenichen, 2007). Even though this is highly debatable, Fair Trade does not improve the situation as the niche speciality market does not focus on the poorest producers.

Fair Trade is responsible for the creation of an additional speciality trade channel, and the institutional system that goes with it probably justifies its claim of promoting a useful social agenda. Fair Trade should restrict itself to this claim and nothing beyond.

Fair Trade and general economic development

Even if we accept Fair Trade's ability to generate some extra benefits for producers and workers, we have to consider that the demand for Fair Trade products is only a limited part of the overall demand for primary products, so the transfer sum available for redistribution is relatively small. The small share of Fair Trade in the overall market limits it to a selected few producers who themselves sell only a fraction of their production to the Fair Trade market. As noted earlier, despite impressive growth in recent years Fair Trade represented only about 0.01 per cent of total food and beverage industry sales worldwide in 2008. Even in the UK, the top Fair Trade consuming market, Fair Trade labelled produce made up less than 0.5 per cent of food and non-alcoholic drinks sales in 2007 (Beattie, 2008). Coffee is the most important Fair Trade commodity, yet its share is surprisingly small even for the top Fair Trade coffee-supplying countries. For example, Costa Rica produced, on average, nearly two million 100-pound bags of coffee each year from 2000 to 2006. Of that, less than 2 per cent was sold as certified Fair Trade coffee; Guatemala's sales of Fair Trade coffee during this period constituted an average of 2.2 per cent of its production (Berndt, 2007).[8]

The impact of Fair Trade is limited not only by the movement's size but also by its narrow scope. The costs and other difficulties in becoming Fair Trade certified are constraints on the expansion of the Fair Trade market and its ability to target the poorest. Therefore, as Fair Trade campaigning and visibility

---

8   Even if we consider all ethical consumer labels we find that they too benefit few producers. Despite the positive attitudes of consumers to ethical consumption, most ethical brands and ethical-label products have a market share of less than 1 per cent (MacGillivray, 2000).

improve, we should not fall prey to picturing it as a panacea to the problem of poverty in underdeveloped countries. At best it is a small part of the solution and should not distract from more comprehensive approaches to poverty reduction. More importantly, Fair Trade should not undermine the benefits from conventional international trade. A report prepared by Ellis and Keane (2008) for the Overseas Development Institute, a London-based think tank, says that there are many exports through conventional markets that are of significant benefit to developing-country producers and which benefit poor farmers to the same extent as exports carrying the Fair Trade mark. The products are not always labelled as Fair Trade, however, as they may not qualify for existing ethical labelling schemes. The report points to a study of green beans purchased from Guatemalan producers by the US retail giant Costco, which benefited poor farming families but were not covered by any of the ethical trading labels (ODI, 2008).

Furthermore, there are many efficient mechanisms within the free market system that can offer special benefits to producers. For example, in the coffee sector some companies have begun to reward producers for supplying sustainable coffee by offering them prices above basic market prices and by offering credit facilities and longer-term contracts. Some producers and producer cooperatives have entered into partnerships with companies to capitalise on the scale and expertise of private export companies. A study of Costa Rican coffee mills suggests that such partnerships have increased prices paid to farmers. At the same time, vertically integrated multinational mills had a similar effect (Ronchi, 2002, 2006).

Also, mobile phones and the Internet provide updated price

and market information to primary producers, which has benefited many of them and allows them to make better production and marketing decisions. There are also possibilities for improving producers' access to futures and options markets to enhance their ability to manage risks arising from variability in price, exchange rates and output.

Therefore, Fair Trade should recognise that it is one of the mechanisms for improving the lot of poor farmers and that it has limited scope. There are other, often more efficient, mechanisms for achieving this objective. Fair Trade's support for marginalised producers, workers and producer and worker unions, or stimulus for producers to reorganise the production process in a socially more acceptable manner, may be worthy ideals, but its proponents should not campaign against or devalue what economists such as Jagdish Bhagwati, Dani Rodrik and Alan Deardorff see as opportunities that international trade offers for development and for improving the conditions of producers and workers in developing countries.

Most of all, Fair Trade should not take the focus away from dealing with the real, long-term solutions of extending free trade and the depth of the market economy. Indeed, given the limited scope of Fair Trade, the main key to reducing poverty is likely to come from other policies to promote development and to remove obstacles to enterprise and trade.

During the recent process of globalisation absolute poverty has decreased dramatically. In China, 300 million people have been pulled out of 'dollar-a-day' poverty in the last decade. It is inconceivable that this would have happened without China's participation in the process of globalisation and free trade. The prospects for other poor countries today depend to a large extent on them ensuring that the basic conditions of good governance exist so that a market economy can flourish.

Indeed, as is noted in Griswold (2009), for nearly the whole of world history until 1800, about 80 per cent of the world's population lived on a subsistence income or below. Then, in 1800, the first phase of globalisation began and, after 150 years, the proportion of the world's population living in dire poverty halved. In the second phase of globalisation, beginning in 1980, the proportion of the world's population living in dire poverty halved again – this time in just 25 years. These achievements resulting from the extension of the market economy based on freer economic exchange and the expansion of global trade have been immense. Also notable is the expansion of the global middle class in the recent phase of globalisation (see Das, 2009) – this is important because there has been huge growth in the number of people in formerly very poor countries who are able to afford not just the necessities of life but also consumer durables and other luxury items while having some income left over to save. For example:

- 70 million people have entered the $6,000–$30,000 a year income band each year in recent years.
- The global middle class is likely to expand to include over one billion now-poor people in developing countries over the next twenty years.
- Defining 'middle class' at a lower level of income – those earning between $2 a day and $13 a day – the middle class rose from 33 per cent of the world's population in 1990 to 49 per cent in 2005 (this implies 1.2 billion people pulled out of poverty – mostly in countries that have embraced globalisation).

It should be added that as well as material living standards improving measures of life expectancy, literacy, infant mortality and more or less every other measure of wellbeing are all improving (see Norberg, 2005).

The Fairtrade Foundation claims that Fair Trade assists 7 million producers, workers and families.[9] This monograph does not seek to undermine that claim nor does it seek to denigrate the importance of Fair Trade as a potential trade channel for particular producers. This number is a drop in the ocean, however, compared with the huge numbers that have been lifted out of poverty as a result of economic liberalisation and the deepening of free trade. Free trade, economic liberalisation and good governance are the keys to substantial reductions in poverty to a much greater extent than the Fair Trade movement can ever be.

Agricultural trade liberalisation

Henderson (2008) opines that a better solution for consumers and Third World producers and workers is to abolish all remaining trade barriers, particularly in agriculture. Trade barriers drive down the net price that foreign producers receive. Many development economists have for years stressed that trade liberalisation has immense benefits that cannot be discarded under the guise of so-called problems caused by or anomalies of free trade. For example, developed-country subsidies and protectionism in agriculture are particularly galling for those countries that have tried to make market reforms work, only to see their producers undercut by subsidised goods in the 'free' world market. The

---

9   http://www.fairtrade.org.uk/get_involved/trade_justice.aspx.

subsidies paid to EU and American farmers directly disadvantage small-scale farmers in underdeveloped countries (Nicholls and Opal, 2005; Mohan, 2007b). They cause overproduction and a lowering of commodity prices. For some commodities such as sugar and cotton it becomes difficult for small-scale farmers to set the terms of trade.

There has been a proliferation of impediments to agricultural trade in both developed and developing economies. According to Aksoy and Beghin (2004), most rich countries impose high tariffs on key domestically produced agricultural products. On top of this, the farming sector in the developed world is able to wring remarkably generous levels of financial support by way of export subsidies and domestic support measures out of their governments. This protectionism is one of the main reasons that developing countries have failed to keep or increase their share of world agricultural exports (Binswanger and Lutz, 1999; Jean et al., 2005; Anderson and Martin, 2005).

OECD (2006) calculates the Producer Support Estimate (PSE) as a measure of overall protection provided to agriculture. The PSE includes both border protection and financial support provided to farmers, expressed as a percentage of gross (support-inclusive) farm receipts. From 2000 to 2003 the PSE was 34 per cent in the EU, 20 per cent in the USA, 58 per cent in Japan and just 4 per cent in Australia. The high PSE values show the level of protection afforded to agriculture in most developed countries. The PSE values are an average for all agriculture products, which means that the protection afforded to certain individual products such as milk, meats, grains and sugar is even higher (OECD, 2005).

Therefore, when it comes to fair trading practices the developed world should lead by example and eliminate its market-distorting agricultural policies. These policies exacerbate poverty in countries and regions such as sub-Saharan Africa, where people are heavily dependent upon agriculture.

It is wrong to think that trade protectionism in agriculture is primarily a developed-country problem – agriculture is also plagued by trade barriers in developing countries.[10] If developing countries want to maximise the benefits to their agricultural producers and workers, they need also to free up their own agricultural markets, particularly for those agricultural products (such as coffee, tea, cocoa, rubber, coconut oil and palm oil) that offer opportunities for the expansion of South–South trade (Mohan, 2007b). For instance, the countries in sub-Saharan Africa would benefit greatly from a lowering of the trade restrictions that they impose against each other (Panagariya, 2005).

Conclusion

The four quotes at the top of the chapter sum up, to a considerable extent, the achievements of and contradictions within the Fair Trade movement.

There is no question that Fair Trade will help some producers – and it may help build more general business capacity that improves the prospects for development more generally within the communities within which it operates. It is a strategy for development that may well help 7 million or more people in this way. It is not, however, a poverty panacea or general long-term development strategy. As we saw in Chapter 4, it is also the case

---

10   The trade barriers in agriculture in developing countries include widespread use of non-tariff restrictions such as import bans, licences or canalising through state agencies (Bureau et al., 2006).

that other labelling initiatives compete in the same space.

It is not 'fair' on the part of Fair Trade or its enthusiasts to promote Fair Trade by undermining conventional international trading practices. On the contrary, they should recognise that conventional trade and certain free market business mechanisms also further the interests of producers and stakeholders through long-term relationships based on mutual respect. Indeed, the capacity for market liberalisation and free trade to lift people out of poverty is an order of magnitude greater than the capacity of Fair Trade. Furthermore, the Fair Trade movement uses strong language to criticise free trade (as in the fourth quote above) while complaining (quite rightly) that existing practices mean that the world's trading system is not free in certain important respects (as in the third quote above). At the same time, the Fair Trade movement campaigns, in effect, for poor countries to keep their restrictions on trade. These lines of reasoning – which are not entirely inconsistent but which are difficult to reconcile with the economic evidence – have made it more difficult for the Fair Trade movement to obtain general approval from free market economists, despite the arguments of Chapter 2 that it is essentially a free market mechanism. This is a pity.

The proponents of Fair Trade would do well to recognise the speciality market characteristics and the costs of Fair Trade, rather than pitch it as a counterweight to the so-called evils of international trade, deregulated markets and the vagaries of the market. Analysts and commentators would then see it from a different perspective, and many of their suspicions and criticisms surrounding it would fade away. Fair Trade would not then be seen as undermining the immense potential of free market trade for improving the economic conditions of producers and workers.

At the same time, opponents of Fair Trade would do well to recognise that it is a niche market mechanism – based on free choice – that can provide help for particular producers in particular circumstances. Nevertheless, it is legitimate, of course, to assess the empirical evidence on the extent of the good (or harm) it does.

6 CONCLUSION

Our analysis of the theory and practice of Fair Trade shows that it is an alternative speciality market trading channel that operates within the free market system. It exists because it satisfies the subjective preference of some consumers who are willing to support it by paying a premium for Fair Trade products. Fair Trade offers opportunities for some producers and workers in developing countries to benefit in terms of income generation, organisational capacity-building and resilience to external shocks in specific situations. It also faces serious practical issues, however, and is not without its costs and limitations.

The organising and managing of the Fair Trade process involves costs of inspection, certification, campaigning for Fair Trade products and maintenance of the Fair Trade bureaucracy. Consequently, a major proportion of the Fair Trade price premium is eaten up, and therefore the net premium actually received by producers is lower than is commonly perceived. The capability of Fair Trade to target marginalised producers is also questionable as its complex entry requirements make it difficult for them to participate and benefit from it. Furthermore, the Fair Trade promotional campaigns tend to convey the impression that free trade is inherently inequitable and anything not carrying the Fair Trade mark was unfairly traded. This is inherently wrong because it fails to recognise that other trading relationships benefit consumers, producers and workers, and at times in less costly ways compared to Fair Trade. It also has the potential to squeeze out other labelling initiatives that are effective in delivering particular social objectives that are desirable to Western consumers.

There are no objective conclusive studies that estimate the benefits and costs of different initiatives. In any case, the emergence of these initiatives should not distract us from the fact that conventional trading too can promote socially responsible practices, including the furthering of interests of producers and stakeholders through long-term relationships based on mutual respect. This can happen without some of the costs and limitations of the private labelling initiatives. Whether Fair Trade actually assists poor producers is an empirical matter. As such, better research on the extent to which Fair Trade helps the really poor and how much of the price enhancement reaches the producer would be welcome.

It is important to recognise that the scope of Fair Trade is limited. This also holds for other social labelling initiatives. As a speciality market movement Fair Trade has a role to play. It has succeeded in forming a small niche market for producers who possibly capture more of the final retail value of their products. Therefore, it can help certain producers and workers in particular circumstances. Fair Trade is not, though, a general, global, long-term development strategy. It should not distract us from the wider issues of trying to facilitate good governance and trade liberalisation. With regard to trade liberalisation, this should include the removal of trade barriers against primary products in the West (supported by the Fair Trade movement) as well as the removal of South–South trade barriers (on which the movement is at best ambiguous).

The advocates of Fair Trade would do well to recognise and promote its speciality market characteristics and not pitch it as a counterweight to the so-called evils of free market international trade. This will result in greater clarity and transparency. Indeed, greater clarity and transparency about the strengths and limitations of Fair Trade would be welcome: the representation of a few particular farmers who have benefited from Fair Trade in promotional materials is unconvincing against a background of 1 billion people living in absolute poverty. Fair Trade needs to decide on the nature and extent of 'mainstream marketing' it should accept without the risk of being attacked for compromising its fundamental principles. Most importantly, Fair Trade should seek to be seen as part of, and not seek to undermine, the immense potential that free trade and liberalised markets offer for improving the economic conditions of producers and workers in underdeveloped countries. Insofar as poverty persists because of the poor environment for business and entrepreneurship that exists in many countries, Fair Trade may be able to help in the economic capacity-building process. As such Fair Trade should seek to complement market liberalisation, freer trade and the development of better governance in poor countries.

REFERENCES

African Fair Trade Symposium Statement (2006), 'Rethinking Fair Trade in Africa – for an African voice in international trade', Cotonou, 6–9 April.

Aksoy, M. A. and J. C. Beghin (eds) (2004), *Global Agricultural Trade and Developing Countries*, Washington, DC: World Bank.

Aldrich, L. (1999), *Consumer Use of Information: Implications for Food Policy*, Agricultural Handbook no. 715, Washington, DC: Food and Rural Economics Division, Economic Research Service, US Department of Agriculture.

Anderson, K. and W. Martin (2005), 'Agricultural trade reform and the Doha development agenda', *World Economy*, 28(9): 1301–27.

Antle, J. M. (1999), 'The new economics for agriculture', *American Journal of Agricultural Economics*, 81: 993–1010.

Bacon, C. (2005), 'Confronting the coffee crisis: can Fair Trade, organic and speciality coffee reduce small-scale farmer vulnerability in northern Nicaragua?', *World Development*, 33(3): 497–511.

Baggini, J. (2007), 'Free doesn't mean unfair', *Guardian*, 5 March, p. 29.

Barrientos, S. and C. Dolan (2006), *Ethical Sourcing in the Global Food System*, London: Earthscan.

Beattie, A. (2008), 'Call for simpler "ethical" labelling', *Financial Times*, 19 November.

Becchetti, L. and F. C. Rosati (2007), 'Global social preferences and the demand for socially responsible products: empirical evidence from a pilot study on Fair Trade consumers', *World Economy*, 30(5): 807–36.

Belgian Science Policy (2005), 'A fair and sustainable trade, between market and solidarity: diagnosis and prospects', Final Report, Brussels: Belgian Science Policy.

Berndt, C. E. H. (2007), 'Does Fair Trade coffee help the poor: evidence from Costa Rica and Guatemala', Mercatus Policy Series, Policy Comment no. 11, Mercatus Center, George Mason University, VA, June.

Binswanger, H. and E. Lutz (1999), *Agricultural Trade Barriers, Trade Negotiations, and the Interest of Developing Countries*, Washington, DC: World Bank.

Black Gold (2006), *A Film about Coffee and Trade*, Warner Bros.

Boot, W., C. Wunderlich and A. Bartra (2003), *Beneficial Impacts of Ecolabeled Mexican Coffee: Organic, Fair Trade, Rainforest Alliance, Bird Friendly*, http://privatizationofrisk.ssrc.org.

Booth, P. (2008), 'The economics of Fairtrade: a Christian perspective', http://www.iea.org.uk.

Booth, P. and L. Whetstone (2007), 'Half a cheer for Fair Trade', *Economic Affairs*, 27(2): 22–30.

Boudreaux, K. (2007), 'State power, entrepreneurship, and coffee: the Rwandan experience', Mercatus Center, George Mason University, VA, September.

Brown, M. B. (1993), *Fair Trade: Reform and Realities in the International Trading System*, London: Zed Books.

Buck, T. (2005), 'More companies reveal social policies', *Financial Times*, 12 July, p. 8.

Bureau, J. C., S. Jean and A. Matthews (2006), 'The consequences of agricultural trade liberalization for developing countries: distinguishing between genuine benefits and false hopes', *World Trade Review*, 5(2): 225–49.

Busch, L. and C. Bain (2004), 'New! Improved? The transformation of the global agrifood system', *Rural Sociology*, 69: 321–46.

Castaldo, S., F. Perrini, N. Misani and A. Tencati (2009), 'The missing link between Corporate Social Responsibility and consumer trust: the case of Fair Trade products', *Journal of Business Ethics*, 84(1): 1–15.

Castle, S. (2006), 'The real price of coffee', *Independent*, 27 October.

Collier, P. (2007), *The Bottom Billion: Why The Poorest Countries are Failing and What Can Be Done About It*, Oxford: Oxford University Press.

COM (2001), 'Promoting a European framework for Corporate Social Responsibility', Green Paper 366 final, Brussels: Commission of the European Communities.

Conroy, M. E. (2001), 'Can advocacy-led certification systems transform global corporate practices? Evidence and some theory', Working Paper no. 21, Amherst: Political Economy Research Institute, University of Massachusetts.

Creyer, E. H. and W. T. Ross (1997), 'The influence of firm behavior on purchase intention: do consumers really care about business ethics?', *Journal of Consumer Marketing*, 14(6): 421–32.

CSRwire (2006), The Corporate Social Responsibility Newswire Service, www.csrwire.com.

Das, D. K. (2009), 'Globalisation and an emerging global middle class', *Economic Affairs*, 29(3): 89–92.

Donaldson, T. and L. E. Preston (1995), 'The stakeholder theory of the corporation: concepts, evidence, and implications', *Academy of Management Review*, 20(1): 65–91.

Economist (2006), 'Voting with your trolley: food politics', Feature article, 7 December.

Economist (2007), 'Excellence in a cup', 25 January.

Ellen, P. S., L. A. Mohr and D. J. Webb (2000), 'Charitable programs and the retailer: do they mix?', *Journal of Retailing*, 76(3): 393–406.

Ellis, K. and J. Keane (2008), 'A review of ethical standards and labels: is there a gap in the market for a new "good for development" label?', ODI Working Paper, London: Overseas Development Institute, November.

Fairtrade Foundation (2006), 'Fairtrade Foundation response to *Financial Times* article' (11 September), http://www.fairtrade. org.uk/ pr110906.htm.

Fairtrade Foundation (2010), 'License fees: wholesale suppliers', http://www.fairtrade.org.uk.

Farnworth, C. and M. Goodman (2006), 'Growing ethical networks: the Fair Trade market for raw and processed agricultural products (in five parts), with associated case studies on Africa and Latin America', Santiago: Rimisp–Latin American Centre for Rural Development, http://www. rimisp.org.

FLO (2006), '2005/2006 annual report: building trust', Fairtrade Labelling Organisations International, http://www.fairtrade. net.

FLO (2007a), '2007 annual report: an inspiration for change', Fairtrade Labelling Organisations International, http://www. fairtrade.net.

FLO (2007b), 'FLO response to *The Economist*', Press release, 28 January, http://www.fairtradewordpress.com.

FLO (2009), 'Growing stronger together: annual report 2009–10', Fairtrade Labelling Organisations International, http://www. fairtrade.net.

FLO-CERT (2010), 'FLO-CERT producer certification fees', Bonn: FLO-CERT GmbH, http://www.flo-cert.net.

Gebben, C. and M. Gitsham (2007), *Food Labelling: Understanding Consumer Attitudes and Behaviour*, Berkhamsted: Ashridge Business School.

Goodman, M. (2007), 'Fair trade', in P. Robbins (ed.), *The Encyclopedia of Environment and Society*, London: Sage.

Griffiths, P. (2009), 'Fairtrade fallacies', http://www. griffithsspeaker.com.

Griffiths, P. (2010), 'Lack of rigour in defending Fair Trade: a reply to Alastair Smith', *Economic Affairs*, 30(2): 45–9.

Griswold, D. T. (2009), *Mad about Trade: Why Main Street America Should Embrace Globalization*, Washington, DC: Cato Institute.

Grodnik, A. and M. E. Conroy (2007), 'Fair Trade coffee in the US', ch. 6 in D. Murray, L. Raynolds and J. Wilkinson (eds), *Fair Trade: The Challenges of Transforming Globalisation*, London: Routledge.

Haight, C. and D. R. Henderson (2010), 'Fair trade is counterproductive and unfair: a rejoinder', *Economic Affairs*, 30(1): 88–91.

Harford, T. (2005), *The Undercover Economist*, Oxford: Oxford University Press.

Hayes, M. (2006), 'On the efficiency of Fair Trade', *Review of Social Economy*, 64(4): 447–68.

✳Henderson, D. R. (2008), 'Fair Trade is counterproductive and unfair', *Economic Affairs*, 28(3): 62–4.

Hiscox, M. J. (2007), 'Fair Trade as an approach to managing globalisation', Memo prepared for Conference on Europe and the Management of Globalisation, Princeton University, 23 February.

Hopkins, R. (2000), 'Impact assessment study of Oxfam Fair Trade', Report, Oxford: Oxfam.

Howley, K. (2006), 'Absolution in your cup', *Reason*, http://www.reason.com, March.

Hughes, A. (2004), 'Accounting for ethical trade: global commodity networks, virtualism, and the audit economy', in S. Reimer and A. Hughes (eds), *Geographies of Commodities*, London: Routledge.

Hughes, A. (2005), 'Corporate strategy and the management of ethical trade: the case of the UK food and clothing retailers', *Environment and Planning A*, 37: 1145–63.

Jacquiau, C. (2006), *Les Coulisses du Commerce Équitable* (Behind the Scenes of Fair Trade), Paris: Éditions Mille et Une Nuits.

Jean, S., D. Laborde and W. Martin (2005), 'Consequences of alternative formulas for agricultural tariff cuts', ch. 4 in K. Anderson and W. Martin (eds), *Agricultural Trade Reform and the Doha Development Agenda*, New York: Palgrave Macmillan.

Karl, H. and C. Orwat (1999), 'Economic aspects of environmental labelling', in H. Former and T. Tietenberg (eds), *The International Year Book of Environmental and Resource Economics*, Cheltenham: Edward Elgar.

Kirchgässner, G. (1992), 'Towards a theory of low-cost decisions', *European Journal of Political Economy*, 8: 305–20.

Kirchgässner, G. and W. W. Pommerehne (1993), 'Low-cost decisions as a challenge to public choice', *Public Choice*, 77: 107–15.

Kohler, P. (2006), 'The economics of Fair Trade: for whose benefit? An investigation into the limits of Fair Trade as a development tool and the risk of clean-washing', HEI Working Papers 06–2007, Geneva: Economics Section, Graduate Institute of International Studies, October.

Krivonos, E. (2004), 'The impact of coffee market reforms on producer prices and price transmission', Policy Research Paper no. 3358, Washington, DC: World Bank.

Leclair, M. S. (2002), 'Fighting the tide: alternative trade organizations in the era of global free trade', *World Development*, 30(6): 949–58.

Lewin, B., D. Giovannucci and P. Varangis (2004), 'Coffee markets: new paradigms in global supply and demand', Agricultural and Rural Development Discussion Paper 3, Washington, DC: World Bank.

Lockie, S. (2006), 'Re-inventing the consumer: food, citizenship and biodiversity', unpublished manuscript.

Lury, C. (2004), *Brands: The Logos of the Global Economy*, New York: Routledge.

Lyon, S. (2006), 'Evaluating Fair Trade consumption: politics, defetishization and producer participation', *International Journal of Consumer Studies*, 30: 452–64.

Lyon, S. (2007), 'Fair Trade coffee and human rights in Guatemala', *J. Consum. Policy*, 30: 241–61.

MacGillivray, A. (2000), *The Fair Share: The Growing Market Share of Green and Ethical Products*, London: New Economics Foundation.

Maizels, A., R. Bacon and G. Mavrotas (1997), *Commodity Supply Management by Producing Countries – a Case-Study of the Tropical Beverage Crops*, Oxford: Clarendon Press.

Marsden, T., J. Banks and G. Bristow (2000), 'Food supply chain approaches: exploring their role in rural development', *Sociologia Ruralis*, 40: 424–38.

Maseland, R. and A. de Vaal (2002), 'How fair is Fair Trade', *De Economist*, 150(3): 251–72.

Mendoza, R. and J. Bastiaensen (2003), 'Fair Trade and the coffee crisis in the Nicaraguan Segovias', *Small Enterprise Development*, 14(2): 36–44.

Mintel (2006), 'Britain becoming a nation of coffee snobs', http://reports.mintel.com/sinatra/reports/display/id=173697/display/id=223313.

Mohan, S. (2005), 'Market-based price-risk management by commodity producers in developing countries: the case of coffee', Doctoral dissertation, University of Strathclyde, Glasgow.

Mohan, S. (2007a), 'Market based price-risk management for coffee producers', *Development Policy Review*, 25(3): 333–54.

Mohan, S. (2007b), 'Reforming agricultural trade among developing countries', *World Trade Review*, 6(3): 397–411.

Mohan, S. and J. Love (2004), 'Coffee futures: role in reducing coffee producers price risk', *Journal of International Development*, 16(7): 983–1002.

Mohan, S. and B. Russell (2008), 'Modelling thirty five years of coffee prices in Brazil, Guatemala and India', Discussion Papers 221, Economic Studies, University of Dundee.

Mohr, L., D. Webb and K. Harris (2001), 'Do consumers expect companies to be socially responsible? The impact of Corporate Social Responsibility on buying behavior', *Journal of Consumer Affairs*, 35(1): 45–72.

Morris, L., M. Hastak and M. Mazis (1995), 'Consumer comprehension of environmental advertising and labelling claims', *Journal of Consumer Affairs*, 29(2): 328–50.

Murdian, R. and W. Pelupessy (2005), 'Governing the coffee chain: the role of voluntary regulatory systems', *World Development*, 33(12): 2029–44.

Murray, D. and L. Raynolds (2007), 'Globalisation and its antinomies: negotiating a Fair Trade movement', ch. 1 in D. Murray, L. Raynolds and J. Wilkinson (eds), *Fair Trade: The Challenges of Transforming Globalisation*, London: Routledge.

Murray, D. L., L. T. Raynolds and P. Taylor (2003), 'One cup at a time: poverty alleviation and Fair Trade coffee in Latin America', Fort Collins: Fair Trade Research Working Group, Colorado State University.

Murray, D. L., L. T. Raynolds and P. Taylor (2006), 'The future of Fair Trade coffee: dilemmas facing Latin America's small-scale producers', *Development in Practice*, 16: 179–92.

Mutersbaugh, T. (2002), 'The number is the best: a political economy of organic-coffee certification and producer unionism', *Environment and Planning A*, 34: 1165–84.

Nelson, V. and P. Pound (2009), *The Last Ten Years: A comprehensive review of the literature on the impact of fair trade*, London: Natural Resources Institute, University of Greenwich.

Nelson, V., A. Tallontire and C. Collison (2002), 'Assessing the benefits of ethical trade schemes for forest dependent people: a comparative experience from Peru and Ecuador', *International Forestry Review*, 4(2): 99–109.

Nicholls, A. and C. Opal (2005), *Fair Trade: Market-Driven Ethical Consumption*, London: Sage.

Norberg, J. (2005), *In Defence of Global Capitalism*, New South Wales: Centre for Independent Studies.

ODI (2008), 'How do ethical and fair trade schemes affect poor producers? Do we need a new "Good for Development" label?', ODI Opinion, London: Overseas Development Institute, November.

OECD (2000), *Guidelines for Multinational Enterprises: Revision 2000*, Paris: Organization for Economic Co-operation and Development, www.oecd.org/daf/investment.

OECD (2005), 'Agricultural policies in OECD countries. Monitoring and evaluation', Paris: Organization for Economic Co-operation and Development.

OECD (2006), 'Review of agricultural policies – China', Paris: Organization for Economic Co-operation and Development.

Oxfam (2002), 'Mugged poverty in your coffee cup', Oxford: Oxfam International.

Panagariya, A. (2005), 'Agricultural liberalizations and the Least Developed Countries: six fallacies', *World Economy*, 28(9): 1277–99.

Pay, E. (2009), 'The market for organic and fair-trade coffee', Study prepared by the Trade and Markets Division, Rome: Food and Agriculture Organisation.

Pelsmacker, P. D. and W. Jansens (2006), 'A model for Fair Trade buying behaviour: the role of perceived quantity and quality of information and of product-specific attitudes', *Journal of Business Ethics*, 75: 361–80.

Porter, M. E. and M. R. Kramer (2006), 'Strategy and society: the link between competitive advantage and Corporate Social Responsibility', *Harvard Business Review*, 84(12): 78–92.

Potts, N. J. (2004), 'Fairness with your coffee?', Auburn, AL: Ludwig von Mises Institute, http://www.mises.org.

Ransom, D. (2005), 'Fair Trade for sale: David Ransom thinks not', *New Internationalist*, April.

Raynolds, L.T. (2002), 'Consumer/producer links in Fair Trade coffee networks', *Sociologia Ruralis*, 42(4): 404–24.

Raynolds, L. T. and M. A. Long (2007), 'Fair/Alternative Trade: historical and empirical dimension', ch. 2 in D. Murray, L. Raynolds and J. Wilkinson (eds), *Fair Trade: The Challenges of Transforming Globalisation*, London: Routledge.

Raynolds, L. T. and D. L. Murray (2007), 'Contemporary challenges and future prospects', ch. 13 in D. Murray, L. Raynolds and J. Wilkinson (eds), *Fair Trade: The Challenges of Transforming Globalisation*, London: Routledge.

Raynolds, L. T. and J. Wilkinson (2007), 'Fair Trade in the agriculture and food sector', ch. 3 in D. Murray, L. Raynolds and J. Wilkinson (eds), *Fair Trade: The Challenges of Transforming Globalisation*, London: Routledge.

Raynolds, L. T., D. L. Murray and P. L. Taylor (2004), 'Fair Trade coffee: building producer capacity via global networks', *Journal of International Development*, 16: 1109–21.

Renard, M. C. (1999), 'The interstices of globalization: the example of fair coffee', *Sociologia Ruralis*, 39(4): 484–500.

Renard, M. C. (2003), 'Fair Trade: quality, market and conventions', *Journal of Rural Studies*, 19(1): 87–96.

Renard, M. C. and V. P. Grovas (2007), 'Fair Trade coffee in Mexico: at the center of the debates', ch. 9 in D. Murray, L. Raynolds and J. Wilkinson (eds), *Fair Trade: The Challenges of Transforming Globalisation*, London: Routledge.

Richardson, M. and F. Stahler (2007), 'Fair Trade', Economics Discussion Paper 0709, University of Otago, New Zealand.

Riedel, C. P., F. M. Lopez, A. Widdows, A. Manji and M. Schneider (2005), 'Impacts of Fair Trade: trade and market linkages', Proceedings of the 18th International Farming Symposium, 31 October–3 November, Rome: Food and Agricultural Organisation, http://www.fao.org/farmingsystems.

Ronchi, L. (2002), 'The impact of Fair Trade on producers and their organizations: a case study with coocafe in Costa Rica', Working Paper No. 11, University of Sussex: Poverty Research Unit.

Ronchi, L. (2006), '"Fairtrade" and market failures in agricultural commodity markets', World Bank Policy Research Working Paper no. 4011, http://econ.worldbank.org, September.

Sellers, F. S. (2005), 'Gift-wrapped guilt?', *Washington Post*, 18 December.

Shreck, A. (2005), 'Resistance, redistribution, and power in the fair trade banana initiative', *Agriculture and Human Values*, 22: 17–29.

Sidwell, M. (2007), *Unfair Trade*, London: Adam Smith Institute.

Singleton, A. (2005), 'The poverty of Fair Trade', London: Adam Smith Institute.

Smith, A. M. (2009), 'Evaluating the criticisms of Fair Trade', *Economic Affairs*, 29(4): 29–36.

Steinrucken, T. and S. Jaenichen (2007), 'The Fair Trade idea: towards an economics of social labels, *J. Consum. Policy*, 30(3): 201–17.

Tallontire, A. and B. Vorley (2005), 'Achieving fairness in trading between supermarkets and their agrofood supply chains', Briefing Paper, London: UK Food Group.

Tallontire, A., E. Rentsendorj and M. Blowfield (2001), 'Consumers and ethical trade: a review of current literature', NRI Policy Series 12, Greenwich: Natural Resources Institute.

Taylor, P. L. (2002), 'Poverty alleviation through participation in Fair Trade coffee networks', Fort Collins: Fair Trade Research Working Group, Colorado State University, September.

Tiffen, P. (2002), 'A chocolate-coated case for alternative international business models', *Development in Practice*, 12(3/4): 383–97.

TransFair USA (2002), Online, http://www.transfairusa.org.

Valkila, J. and A. Nygren (2009), 'Impacts of Fair Trade certification on coffee farmers, cooperatives, and laborers in Nicaragua', *Agriculture and Human Values*, 27(3): 321–33.

Varian, H. R. (2003), *Intermediate Microeconomics*, 6th edn, New York: Norton.

Webb, J. (2007), 'Seduced or sceptical consumers? Organised action and the case of Fair Trade coffee', *Sociological Research Online*, 12(3), http://www.socresonline.org.uk/12/3/5.html.

Weber, J. (2006), 'Rationing in the Fair Trade coffee market: who enters and how?', Paper presented at the 'Second International Colloquium: Fair Trade and Sustainable Development', University of Quebec, Montreal, 19–21 June.

Weber, J. (2007), 'Fair Trade coffee enthusiasts should confront reality', *Cato Journal*, 27(1): 109–17.

Weitzman, H. (2006), 'The bitter cost of "Fair Trade" coffee', *Financial Times*, 8 September.

Wilkinson, J. (2007), 'Fair Trade: dynamics and dilemmas of a market oriented global social movement', *J. Consum. Policy*, 30(2): 219–39.

Wilkinson, J. and G. Mascarenhas (2007), 'Southern social movements and Fair Trade', ch. 8 in D. Murray, L. Raynolds and J. Wilkinson (eds), *Fair Trade: The Challenges of Transforming Globalisation*, London: Routledge.

Zadek, S. and P. Tiffin (1996), 'Fair Trade: business or campaign?', *Development: Journal of the Society for International Development*, 3: 48–53.

ABOUT THE IEA

The Institute is a research and educational charity (No. CC 235 351), limited by guarantee. Its mission is to improve understanding of the fundamental institutions of a free society by analysing and expounding the role of markets in solving economic and social problems.

The IEA achieves its mission by:

- a high-quality publishing programme
- conferences, seminars, lectures and other events
- outreach to school and college students
- brokering media introductions and appearances

The IEA, which was established in 1955 by the late Sir Antony Fisher, is an educational charity, not a political organisation. It is independent of any political party or group and does not carry on activities intended to affect support for any political party or candidate in any election or referendum, or at any other time. It is financed by sales of publications, conference fees and voluntary donations.

In addition to its main series of publications the IEA also publishes a quarterly journal, *Economic Affairs*.

The IEA is aided in its work by a distinguished international Academic Advisory Council and an eminent panel of Honorary Fellows. Together with other academics, they review prospective IEA publications, their comments being passed on anonymously to authors. All IEA papers are therefore subject to the same rigorous independent refereeing process as used by leading academic journals.

IEA publications enjoy widespread classroom use and course adoptions in schools and universities. They are also sold throughout the world and often translated/reprinted.

Since 1974 the IEA has helped to create a worldwide network of 100 similar institutions in over 70 countries. They are all independent but share the IEA's mission.

Views expressed in the IEA's publications are those of the authors, not those of the Institute (which has no corporate view), its Managing Trustees, Academic Advisory Council members or senior staff.

Members of the Institute's Academic Advisory Council, Honorary Fellows, Trustees and Staff are listed on the following page.

The Institute gratefully acknowledges financial support for its publications programme and other work from a generous benefaction by the late Alec and Beryl Warren.

Other papers recently published by the IEA include:

Towards a Liberal Utopia?
Edited by Philip Booth
Hobart Paperback 32; ISBN 0 255 36563 2; £15.00

The Way Out of the Pensions Quagmire
Philip Booth & Deborah Cooper
Research Monograph 60; ISBN 0 255 36517 9; £12.50

Black Wednesday
A Re-examination of Britain's Experience in the Exchange Rate Mechanism
Alan Budd
Occasional Paper 135; ISBN 0 255 36566 7; £7.50

Crime: Economic Incentives and Social Networks
Paul Ormerod
Hobart Paper 151; ISBN 0 255 36554 3; £10.00

The Road to Serfdom *with* **The Intellectuals and Socialism**
Friedrich A. Hayek
Occasional Paper 136; ISBN 0 255 36576 4; £10.00

Money and Asset Prices in Boom and Bust
Tim Congdon
Hobart Paper 152; ISBN 0 255 36570 5; £10.00

The Dangers of Bus Re-regulation
and Other Perspectives on Markets in Transport
John Hibbs et al.
Occasional Paper 137; ISBN 0 255 36572 1; £10.00

The New Rural Economy
Change, Dynamism and Government Policy
Berkeley Hill et al.
Occasional Paper 138; ISBN 0 255 36546 2; £15.00

The Benefits of Tax Competition
Richard Teather
Hobart Paper 153; ISBN 0 255 36569 1; £12.50

Wheels of Fortune
Self-funding Infrastructure and the Free Market Case for a Land Tax
Fred Harrison
Hobart Paper 154; ISBN 0 255 36589 6; £12.50

Were 364 Economists All Wrong?
Edited by Philip Booth
Readings 60; ISBN 978 0 255 36588 8; £10.00

Europe After the 'No' Votes
Mapping a New Economic Path
Patrick A. Messerlin
Occasional Paper 139; ISBN 978 0 255 36580 2; £10.00

The Railways, the Market and the Government
John Hibbs et al.
Readings 61; ISBN 978 0 255 36567 3; £12.50

Corruption: The World's Big C
Cases, Causes, Consequences, Cures
Ian Senior
Research Monograph 61; ISBN 978 0 255 36571 0; £12.50

Choice and the End of Social Housing
Peter King
Hobart Paper 155; ISBN 978 0 255 36568 0; £10.00

Sir Humphrey's Legacy
Facing Up to the Cost of Public Sector Pensions
Neil Record
Hobart Paper 156; ISBN 978 0 255 36578 9; £10.00

The Economics of Law
Cento Veljanovski
Second edition
Hobart Paper 157; ISBN 978 0 255 36561 1; £12.50

Living with Leviathan
Public Spending, Taxes and Economic Performance
David B. Smith
Hobart Paper 158; ISBN 978 0 255 36579 6; £12.50

The Vote Motive
Gordon Tullock
New edition
Hobart Paperback 33; ISBN 978 0 255 36577 2; £10.00

Waging the War of Ideas
John Blundell
Third edition
Occasional Paper 131; ISBN 978 0 255 36606 9; £12.50

The War Between the State and the Family
How Government Divides and Impoverishes
Patricia Morgan
Hobart Paper 159; ISBN 978 0 255 36596 3; £10.00

Capitalism – A Condensed Version
Arthur Seldon
Occasional Paper 140; ISBN 978 0 255 36598 7; £7.50

Catholic Social Teaching and the Market Economy
Edited by Philip Booth
Hobart Paperback 34; ISBN 978 0 255 36581 9; £15.00

Adam Smith – A Primer
Eamonn Butler
Occasional Paper 141; ISBN 978 0 255 36608 3; £7.50

Happiness, Economics and Public Policy
Helen Johns & Paul Ormerod
Research Monograph 62; ISBN 978 0 255 36600 7; £10.00

They Meant Well
Government Project Disasters
D. R. Myddelton
Hobart Paper 160; ISBN 978 0 255 36601 4; £12.50

Rescuing Social Capital from Social Democracy
John Meadowcroft & Mark Pennington
Hobart Paper 161; ISBN 978 0 255 36592 5; £10.00

Paths to Property
Approaches to Institutional Change in International Development
Karol Boudreaux & Paul Dragos Aligica
Hobart Paper 162; ISBN 978 0 255 36582 6; £10.00

Prohibitions
Edited by John Meadowcroft
Hobart Paperback 35; ISBN 978 0 255 36585 7; £15.00

Trade Policy, New Century
The WTO, FTAs and Asia Rising
Razeen Sally
Hobart Paper 163; ISBN 978 0 255 36544 4; £12.50

Sixty Years On – Who Cares for the NHS?
Helen Evans
Research Monograph 63; ISBN 978 0 255 36611 3; £10.00

Taming Leviathan
Waging the War of Ideas Around the World
Edited by Colleen Dyble
Occasional Paper 142; ISBN 978 0 255 36607 6; £12.50

Taxation and Red Tape
The Cost to British Business of Complying with the UK Tax System
Francis Chittenden, Hilary Foster & Brian Sloan
Research Monograph 64; ISBN 978 0 255 36612 0; £12.50

Ludwig von Mises – A Primer
Eamonn Butler
Occasional Paper 143; ISBN 978 0 255 36629 8; £7.50

Does Britain Need a Financial Regulator?
Statutory Regulation, Private Regulation and Financial Markets
Terry Arthur & Philip Booth
Hobart Paper 169; ISBN 978 0 255 36593 2, £12.50

Hayek's *The Constitution of Liberty*
An Account of Its Argument
Eugene F. Miller
Occasional Paper 144; ISBN 978 0 255 36637 3; £12.50

Other IEA publications

Comprehensive information on other publications and the wider work of the IEA can be found at www.iea.org.uk. To order any publication please see below.

Personal customers

Orders from personal customers should be directed to the IEA:
Sam Collins
IEA
2 Lord North Street
FREEPOST LON10168
London SW1P 3YZ
Tel: 020 7799 8907. Fax: 020 7799 2137
Email: scollins@iea.org.uk

Trade customers

All orders from the book trade should be directed to the IEA's distributor:
Gazelle Book Services Ltd (IEA Orders)
FREEPOST RLYS-EAHU-YSCZ
White Cross Mills
Hightown
Lancaster LA1 4XS
Tel: 01524 68765. Fax: 01524 53232
Email: sales@gazellebooks.co.uk

IEA subscriptions

The IEA also offers a subscription service to its publications. For a single annual payment (currently £42.00 in the UK), subscribers receive every monograph the IEA publishes. For more information please contact:
Sam Collins
Subscriptions
IEA
2 Lord North Street
FREEPOST LON10168
London SW1P 3YZ
Tel: 020 7799 8907. Fax: 020 7799 2137
Email: scollins@iea.org.uk